The Unofficial Guide to The Scorpion King and The Mummy Universe

By Brad Mengel

Published in the USA by
BearManor Media
1317 Edgewater Dr. #110
Orlando, FL 32804
www.BearManorMedia.com

Softcover Edition
ISBN-10:
ISBN-13: 979-8-88771-074-7

Printed in the United States of America

Dedication:

To Mark Mandell, Nancy Holder, Chris Sequeira and Marv Wolfman
for their advice and support for this project.

Contents

Contents

Contents

Contents

"Death is only the Beginning"

Introduction by Brad Mengel

In 1999, Universal released a reboot of *The Mummy* (1932). Also titled *The Mummy*, it starred Brendan Fraser, Rachel Weisz and Arnold Vosloo and blended the horror of the original with the swashbuckling heroics of Indiana Jones. It entered the public consciousness as the Brendan Fraser Mummy. Over 20 years later and people are still talking about this film.

The film was a success and spawned a franchise. There were video games, comics, books, and more movies, it even created its own spinoff franchise with *The Scorpion King* which launched the acting career of Dwayne "The Rock" Johnson.

I was hooked from that first Mummy movie, which became my go to when there was nothing else to watch. I saw the three Mummy movies (and the Scorpion King) in the cinema and was excited to see the set up for another movie in the series at the end of *The Mummy: Tomb of the Dragon Emperor* (2008).

That fourth movie was not to be. The third movie didn't perform to expectations and in 2012, Universal announced plans for a modern-day reboot of *The Mummy*, which was intended to be the launching point of The Dark Universe cinematic universe.

The 1999 Mummy franchise was the victim of the Dark Universe but a DVD exclusive tie-in for the third movie gave The Scorpion King franchise fresh life, with the release of *The Scorpion King 2: Rise of a Warrior* (2008), a prequel to the 2002 movie. More DVD exclusive movies followed in 2012 and 2015.

With the release of The Dark Universe Mummy in 2017, many assumed that was the end for the Scorpion King but 2018 saw the release of a fifth Scorpion King movie – *Scorpion King: Book of Souls*. There was still hope. Then in November 2020, Dwayne Johnson announced that he was producing a modern-day reboot of *The Scorpion King*. That seemed to be the end of Scorpion King franchise.

With the end of the Scorpion King/Mummy franchise, I decided I was going to do a rewatch/reread. Except there was no guide for the entire franchise. There was no complete timeline, no companion to show me the beasts and monsters encountered, or the relics and artefacts found by our explorers. You know what they say, if you can't find what you want to read – write it yourself.

How to Use the Guide

This book covers the three *Mummy* movies, the five *Scorpion King* movies, the 13 episodes of *The Mummy: The Animated Series* and the 13 episodes of the second season retitled *The Mummy: The Secrets of the Medjai*, seven comic issues across three miniseries, four original junior novels and the various tie-novelizations and adaptations. Due to the variety of formats and media, each entry will be referred to as an Adventure.

Names that are only spoken and the spelling is uncertain will be marked with ★.

I have standardized the spelling of names and places throughout this book, for example: Medjai has been written as Med Jai and Med-Jai in various sources. As the second season of the animated series was subtitled "*Secrets of the Medjai*" and I have adopted that spelling.

The format of each entry is as follows:

TITLE

Date of Release:

Cast

Writer

Director

Don't I Know You?: The various adventures had appearances from wrestlers, MMA fighters, and actors from other productions.

Historical Backstory: The story often has a historical exploit or background before the main adventure.

Plot Summary: A summary of the adventure's plot.

Past Lives: When details are given about the past of any of the leads.

Where in the World: The adventure's location. *The Mummy: The Animated Series* tends to do a great deal of globe hopping.

Bestiary: Gods and monsters encountered in the adventures.

Reliquary: Any relics or artefacts found in the adventure.

No Harm Ever Came From Reading a Book: Changes between the events on screen and the adaptations.

Take That Bembridge Scholars!: Where the past has been retconned and changed.

Notes: Any other notes on the adventures.

Before The Mummy (1999):

A Brief History of the Mummy Movie

Stories of animated mummies date back to ancient times with tales from 19th Dynasty of Ancient Egypt ("Khaemwaset and the Mummies" retold by Herodotus) and are far too many for this guide. A who's who of writers have added to mummy fiction: Edgar Allan Poe; Sir Arthur Conan Doyle; Guy Boothby; Bram Stoker; and Louisa May Alcott to name a few.

With discovery of Tutankhamun's tomb in 1923, the pulp magazines were filled with Mummy stories. Harry Houdini with H.P Lovecraft, Frank Belknap Long, Robert Bloch and many other pulpsters wrote about mummies.

The Mummy did not move to the screen so well. "The Mummy's Foot" (1840) by Theophile Gaultier formed the basis of the one of earliest mummy films *The Haunted Curiosity Shop* (1901). Unlike *Dracula* (1897) or *Frankenstein* (1818), there was no great mummy tale to become a blockbuster film. Although as we will see Bram Stoker's *Jewel of the Seven Stars* (1903 and revised in 1912) has been filmed several times.

The Universal movies

The Mummy 1932

In 1932, Universal Studies sought to follow up the success of *Dracula* (1931) starring Bela Lugosi and *Frankenstein* (1931) starring Boris Karloff, started production on a script titled *Cagliostro* about an immortal Egyptian magician of that name. In rewrites, the script changed –gone was Cagliostro and in his place Im-Ho-Tep and the title changed to *The Mummy*.

Karloff took the role of Im-Ho-Tep, who an ancient Egyptian cursed for his love of the Princess Anck-es-en-Amon and the theft of the Scroll of Thoth he was using to try and bring her back from the dead. Some say that Im-Ho-Tep is one of Karloff's best roles.

Im-Ho-Tep's mummy was uncovered by Sir Joseph Whemple in a 1921 prologue and the resurrected mummy using the alias Ardath Bey encountered Sir Joseph's son, Frank, along with their occultist friend Dr Muller battling over the reincarnation of Anck-es-en-Amon.

The Kharis movies

The Mummy Legacy Collection

Unlike *Dracula* (1931) and *Frankenstein* (1931), *The Mummy* (1932) had no sequels. When Universal next made a mummy movie *The Mummy's Hand* (1940), it was about a new mummy, Kharis. With a plot (and some footage) borrowed from Karloff's movie, the story revolved around cursed love affair between Kharis and Princess Ananka. The Whemples were replaced by Steve Banning and his son John battling the resurrected mummy.

In this case, rather than a curse Kharis was kept alive through the use of Tana leaves by the High Priests of Karnak to serve eternally as Ananka's guardian. In *The Mummy's Hand* (1940), Kharis was played by former Olympian Tom Tyler who would go on to play Captain Marvel and The Phantom in serials. For the next three movies *The Mummy's Tomb* (1942), *The Mummy's Ghost (1944)* and *The Mummy's Curse (1944)* the role of Kharis was taken by Lon Chaney Jnr, who had previously played the son of Dracula, the Frankenstein's Monster and The Wolfman in other Universal movies.

Abbott and Costello meet the Mummy

At the end of the horror movie cycle where Universal had their monsters Dracula, Frankenstein's Monster and the Wolfman meet and fight, the decision was made to have the monsters meet comedy stars Bud Abbott and Lou Costello in the horror–comedy *Abbott and Costello Meet Frankenstein (1948)*. The success of this leads the comedy duo made several more horror comedies *Abbott and Costello meet the Killer Boris Karloff (1949)* with Boris Karloff, *Abbott and Costello meet The Invisible Man (1951)*, *Abbott and Costello meet Dr. Jekyll and Mr. Hyde (1953)*. The final classic Universal Mummy movie and the last film Abbott and Costello made together was *Abbott and Costello Meet the Mummy (1955)*. The comics become involved in a search for treasure and encounter a resurrected mummy, Klaris.

Hammer Time

After the end of the classic Universal Monster cycle, British studio Hammer sought to reinvigorate the genre with full color reinterpretations of the classic monsters *The Curse of Frankenstein* (1957) and *Dracula* aka *The Horror of Dracula* (1958) both starring Christopher Lee and Peter Cushing.

The Mummy (1959) Poster

Both movies were distributed in the United States by Universal. The movies were so successful that they saved Universal from bankruptcy and the head of Universal was so pleased that meeting with representatives from Hammer, he offered them the remake rights to any of the Universal properties. Contemporary reports indicate that Hammer selected *The Invisible Man*, which was never made, *The Phantom of the Opera*, which Hammer didn't make until 1962 and *The Mummy (1959)*.

The Hammer Mummy borrowed from the Kharis cycle of movies, resurrecting that mummy, played by Christopher Lee, along with the Banning family of archaeologists with Peter Cushing as John.

While *The Mummy* (1959) was success, it was four years before they made another Mummy movie, *The Curse of the Mummy's Tomb* (1964). This was not a continuation of the first film but the story of resurrected Mummy RaAntef and his vengeance against those who defiled his tomb and the reveal that one member of the party has a connection to the mummy.

Two years later, Hammer made another Mummy film, *The Mummy's Shroud* (1966) which deals with discovery of the mummy of Prince

Kah-to-Bey and resurrection of his protector Prem to avenge his prince.

The final Hammer Mummy film *Blood from the Mummy's Tomb* (1971) was the first film version Bram Stoker's novel *Jewel of the Seven Stars* (1903 and revised in 1912). It had previously been adapted as "Curse of the Mummy" the final episode of the TV series *Mystery and Imagination* a year earlier. It would form the basis for at least three other versions *The Awakening* (1980), *Bram Stoker's Legend of the Mummy* (1997) and *The Mummy Resurrected* (2014).

The Universal Love Letter

The Monster Squad (1987)

In 1987, *The Monster Squad* was released. The story revolved around a gang of kids who love monster movies facing down Dracula and his army of monsters, the Frankenstein's Monster, a werewolf, a gill-man, and a mummy. Reportedly the film's director Fred Decker and the writer Shane Black approached Universal to make the film, but they passed. This monster mash of a movie featured an unnamed mummy, in homage to Kharis was a bandaged, shuffling monster. He was creatively destroyed with a bow and arrow.

There were reports that after *The Mummy: Tomb of the Dragon Emperor* (2008), director Rob Cohen was looking to remake this movie.

The Return of the Universal

In 1992, the earliest attempt at revitalizing the Mummy began and horror writer Clive Barker was brought into to write and direct. He wrote a script with Mick Garris (director of *Critters 2* (1988) and *Psycho IV: The Beginning* (1990)). Based on interviews, the movie opens with the portentous birth of a baby boy. We then leap forward 20 years to modern times, and we follow a high society cult seeking to resurrect the Mummy. The cult is infiltrated by a seductive woman, with twist being that the baby is now grown up as this transgender woman. Reportedly, Universal hated it and rejected the script outright. In a 2021 podcast with Garris, Barker stated that he still wanted to make this film and suggested that they talk to Netflix.

Joe Dante had a script by Alan Ormsby with revisions by John Sayles. Reports indicate that Daniel Day-Lewis was attached to play the Mummy and other reports had Christopher Lee, who Dante worked with in *Gremlins 2: A New Batch* (1990) on board to play the mummy. Steven Spielberg championed the script to Universal, but they passed. Reportedly, the studio did not want a contemporary story but rather a period piece.

George A Romero was brought in 1994, his plot had Egyptologist Helen Grosvenor unknowingly resurrecting Imhotep while scanning his mummy in an MRI scanner. The energy restores Imhotep to his youthful body and pair begin a romance. Using his magic, Imhotep resurrects his servant Kharis who was buried with him to attack the looters and collectors who robbed their tomb. Reports indicate that Universal passed on this script as it would have been too expensive, and they felt it was too dark.

Then in 1997, Universal bought in Stephen Sommers and the rest is history.

High Adventure!

The Mummy (1999) is not just a horror movie, it blends the horror of the classic mummy with the tropes of adventure genre.

The genre was largely re-popularized by the success of *Raiders of the Lost Ark* (1981) which introduced Indiana Jones. *The Mummy* (1999) took the template of Raiders and went a step further with Rick O'Connell and Evelyn O'Connell sharing the "Indy" role – Evelyn being the intellectual "archaeologist" and Rick the adventurer.

While Indy hunted for religious artefacts that had some supernatural abilities (The Ark of the Covenant, the Sankara Stones, the Holy Grail and the Crystal Skulls) he did so against human enemies, Nazis (twice), Kali Cultists and Soviets, with the supernatural powers only coming into play at the end of the adventure. In *The Mummy* (1999), not only did the Carnahan party have race against a rival archaeological dig but the supernatural entity, the Mummy, comes to life and challenges the heroes. This challenge is so much that the rivalry between the two dig teams is forgotten, and they team up against the Mummy.

Just as much as its horror roots in other mummy movies, *The Mummy* (1999) uses many of the tropes of adventure fiction.

The Adventuring Archaeologist

Tales of hunts for lost treasures and the people hunting them have been a staple of the adventure genre for years. There were books such as *King Solomon's Mines* (1885), and *Treasure Island* (1883). The discovery of King Tutankhamen in 1922, gave the field of archaeology a greater place in the cultural zeitgeist and we see archaeologists appear in the Doc Savage pulp series, the movies *Pimpernel Smith* (1941), *Valley of the Sun* (1942) and *The Secret of the Incas* (1954).

Comic book superheroes like Hawkman (Carter Hall), Blue Beetle (Dan Garrett) and Metamorpho (Rex Mason) were all archaeologists in their civilian identities. The movie serial version of *Captain Marvel* (1941) has Billy Batson being granted his powers during an archaeological dig and battling a rogue member of the dig team who is trying to use the mystic artefact for his own benefit.

The genre went through a renaissance with the Indiana Jones movies starting in 1981 with movies like *Firewalker* (1986) and *Armor of God* (1986) and book series such as *The Takers* (1984) by Jerry and Sharon Ahern and *Lincoln Blackthorne* (1984) by Geoffrey Marsh (Charles L. Grant) all appearing to cash in on the success. In 1996, the video game *Tomb Raider* appeared in the first of several adventures of Lara Croft, a globetrotting freelance archaeologist.

The Mummy (1999) expanded the role of the archaeologists from the original 1932 movie that it was remaking using the template popularized by Indiana Jones and various adventurers making an adventure horror genre crossover.

The Legionnaire

The French Foreign Legion was a romantic fantasy – men who left their old life behind seeking a new start in the Legion serving in the exotic Middle East. Arguably popularized by P.C. Wren's novel *Beau Geste* (1924) and several sequels and adaptations, the Legion was a stable of adventure fiction appearing in many adventure stories including Philip Wylie's *Gladiator* (1930), *Adventure in the Sahara* (1938), *Captain Gallant of the Foreign Legion* (1955) and more recently in films *Legionnaire* (1998) and *Secondhand Lions* (2003).

While Indiana Jones doesn't join the Foreign Legion, during *The Young Indiana Jones Chronicles* Episode "London, May 1916" (edited into the TV movie *Love's Sweet Song*) , Indy initially joins the Belgian Army under the alias Henri Defense during World War One. The use of an alias and adventures in Africa uses all the tropes of a Foreign Legion story.

After the backstory of Imhotep's mummification in 1290BC, *The Mummy* opens in 1923 with a battalion of French Foreign Legionnaires fighting off numerous Bedouins and we are introduced to both Rick

O'Connell and Beni Gabor, who play a major role in the remainder of the movie.

We are reminded on Rick's Legionnaire background in *The Mummy: Tomb of the Dragon Emperor* (2008), with a brief scene showing his Legion uniform and meeting up with Rick's old Legion pilot buddy Maddog Maguire, who helps the O'Connell family flying them around in that adventure.

The Cowboy

The history of the Western is far too long to go into here but since the days of the dime novel which mythologized historical figures like Calamity Jane, Wyatt Earp, Billy the Kid and Jesse James and created fictional cowboys, the cowboy riding the wild west solving problems with his six shooters has been very popular.

The Mummy (1999) transplants the cowboy to Egypt. At the start of the 1926 portion of the movie Jonathan refers to Rick as a cowboy. Rick appears with a bag full of weapons including several revolvers and rifles.

However the rival American party gives us a more distilled version of the cowboy with their three American members, Burns, Henderson, and Daniels. All three sport revolvers with Henderson and Daniels both sport Colt Single Action Quick Draws and we see Henderson, who dresses most like a traditional cowboy, practicing his quick draw while waiting for Imhotep to attack. All three men are quick on the trigger, yelling "yeehaw" and sending a hail of bullets at the Medjai who attack the boat heading down the Nile.

The Aviator

With the invention of the airplane in 1903, flying became a new frontier of adventure. The aerial battles of World War One and later long distance flying feats of Charles Lindberg and Amelia Earhart made aviators heroes. The aviation pulps like Biggles, G-8, the Red Falcon, and Bill Barnes further cemented the heroics of pilots. This trend followed with more modern comic book adventures like Air Hawk, Blackhawk, Airboy, Ace Drummond, Captain Midnight, and the Rocketeer.

The Mummy series features several Aviator allies for the O'Connells. The retired World War One aviator Winston Havlock in *The Mummy*, Rick's pilot friend Izzy in *The Mummy Returns* (2001) and Maddog Maguire in *The Mummy: Tomb of the Dragon Emperor* (2008).

The Mummy animated series (2001–2003) had the O'Connells flying their own dirigible, the Zephyr, around the world. The episode "Trio" revealed that part of Ardeth Bay's modernization of the Medjai is the purchase of a plane that Alex and his fellow students use to follow Imhotep and foil his plan.

The Mummy (1999) is a movie that movies beyond its horror origins as remake of the 1932 original and utilizes the adventure tropes utilized and reinvigorated by Indiana Jones and those who followed in his footsteps.

The Mummy

The Mummy (1999)

Release Date: June 24, 1999

The Cast:

Brendan Fraser ....Rick O'Connell

Rachel Weisz ....Evelyn Carnahan

John Hannah ....Jonathan Carnahan

Arnold Vosloo ....Imhotep

Kevin J O'Connor .....Beni Gabor

Oded Fehr ....Ardeth Bay

Erick Avari ....Dr Terrence Bey (the Curator)

Jonathan Hyde ....Dr Allen Chamberlain (the Egyptologist)

Stephen Durham ......Mr. Henderson

Corey Johnson ....Mr. Daniels

Tuc Watkins ....Mr. Burns

Bernard Fox ....Capt. Winston Havlock

Patricia Velasquez ...Anck-Su-Namun

Aharon Ipale ....Pharaoh Seti I

Writer/Director: Stephen Sommers.

Don't I know you?:

Brendan Fraser: This leading man appeared in many movies including *Encino Man* (1992), *George of the Jungle* (1997), *Bedazzled* (2000), *Looney Tunes: Back in Action* (2003), *Inkheart* (2008), *Journey to the Centre of the Earth* (2008) and Robotman in *Doom Patrol* (2019).

Rachel Weisz: Won an Oscar for *The Constant Gardner* (2005) as well as appearing in *Constantine* (2005), *Eragon* (2006) and *Black Widow* (2021).

John Hannah: Appeared in *Spartacus* (2010-2013) and *Agents of SHIELD* (2013-2020) as well as the movies *Four Weddings and a Funeral* (1994) and *Sliding Doors* (1998).

Arnold Vosloo: This South African actor appeared as Darkman in the Direct to DVD sequels *Darkman II: The Return of Durant* (1995) and *Darkman III: Die, Darkman, Die* (1996). He later appeared as Vincent in *Veritas: The Quest* (2003-2004).

Kevin J. O'Connor: A frequent collaborator with director Stephen Sommers, he has appeared in *Deep Rising* (1998), *Van Helsing* (2004) and *GI Joe: The Rise of Cobra* (2009).

Oded Fehr: Since the Mummy, Fehr has appeared in several TV series *UC Undercover* (2001-2002), *Blood & Treasure* (2019), and as a series regular in season 3 of *Star Trek: Discovery* (2017). He also provided the voice for N'Kantu, The Living Mummy in the animated series *Ultimate Spider-Man* (2012-2017) and *Hulk and the Agents of S.M.A.S.H.* (2013-2015).

Erick Avari: One of only two actors to appear in both the *Stargate* movie and the spinoff series *Stargate SG1*, Avari has a long list of acting credits including appearing in episodes of both *Leverage* and *Castle* that deal with a mummy's curse.

Bernard Fox: This Welsh actor had starred in many film and TV productions but was best known for the role of Doctor Bombay, the Witch Doctor in *Bewitched* (1964-1972).

Stephen Sommers: Wrote and directed *The Jungle Book* (1994), *Deep Rising* (1998), *Van Helsing* (2004), *G.I. Joe: The Rise of Cobra* (2009) and *Odd Thomas* (2013).

Historical Backstory:

1290 BC - In Thebes, the city of the living, the high priest Imhotep is caught in a relationship with Anck-Su-Namun, the mistress of Pharaoh Seti I. The pair slay the pharaoh and Imhotep flees as Anck-Su-Namun kills herself before the Medjai, the Pharaoh's bodyguard.

Imhotep steals her body and races to Hamunaptra, the city of the dead, to resurrect her with his fellow priests. They are captured by Medjai, and the priests are mummified alive.

Imhotep is cursed with the Hom-dai – an eternal life to be tortured and eaten by scarab beetles.

Plot Summary

1923 Battle of Hamunaptra. The French Foreign Legion garrison of Corporal Rick O'Connell has marched from Libya to Egypt after the discovery of a map to Hamunaptra, the city of the dead where Seti I was rumored to store his treasure. Upon arrival the Legionnaires are attacked by Tuaregs. Most of the Legionnaires are killed in the battle before the Tuaregs flee in terror as a giant face appears in the sand. The Medjai watch the battle and as Rick flees Hamunaptra, they don't kill him as they believe the desert will get him.

Three Years Later (1926) Librarian Evelyn Carnahan, the daughter of noted Egyptologist Howard Carnahan and his Egyptian wife, is visited by her older brother Jonathan. He has discovered a puzzle box which contains a map to Hamunaptra.

After the map is burnt by Evelyn's boss Dr Terrence Bey, it is revealed that Jonathan has picked Rick's pocket for the puzzle box at the bar the night before.

The Carnahan siblings visit Rick in jail, where he was thrown after having a good time the night before. Rick recognizes and punches Jonathan before he offers to lead them to Hamunaptra if they can get him out of jail. Evy negotiates with warden as Rick is being hung. The pair come to terms just in time to save Rick's life.

The next morning, the Carnahans are joined by Rick and the warden on a boat heading down the Nile. The group discovers another party consisting of Egyptologist Dr Allen Chamberlin and three American adventurers, Burns, Daniels, and Henderson are also on board. Rick discovers that the rival party are being guided Beni, Rick's old Legionnaire buddy, who also survived the battle three years earlier.

Despite the setback of an attack on their ship by the Medjai, both parties make it to Hamunaptra and begin digging. The Chamberlin party discovers the black Book of the Dead and Canopic jars, while the Carnahan party finds the sarcophagus containing the cursed remains of Imhotep.

Despite a warning to leave from Ardeth Bay of the Medjai, the dig continues. Evy reads from the Book of the Dead, that she has surreptitiously borrowed from the other party, and awakens the mummy and unleashes a plague of locusts. As the parties flee they encounter the mummy, who steals Burns' eyes and tongue. Imhotep mistakes Evy for his lover Anck-Su-Namun but Rick blasts the mummy with his shotgun. The Medjai rescue both parties who return to Cairo, but Beni is left behind and makes a deal to serve Imhotep.

Back in Cairo at Fort Brydon, the men are all ready to leave but Evy wants to try and stop the mummy. More plagues strike the city including turning water into blood. Imhotep kills Burns and tries to steal Evy. Rick chases Imhotep away with a white cat and the surviving party visits Dr Bey. They find him talking with Ardeth Bay, revealing that the curator is one of the Medjai. They pool information and discover that the golden book of Amun-Ra is the key to stopping Imhotep.

The mummy kills the rest of Chamberlin's party restoring his body and his full powers. After a standoff Imhotep abducts Evy sweeping her off to Hamunaptra. Rick, Jonathan, and Ardeth Bay follow in a biplane flown by Winston Havlock, a WWI veteran.

Imhotep attacks the plane with a sandstorm causing the plane to crash. He then takes Evy into Hamunaptra to use her to resurrect Anck-Su-Namun. During this Beni explores the city and discovers the treasure room. In his greed, Beni makes several runs, loading up a camel with treasure. On his last run, he accidentally pulls a lever that causes Hamunaptra to sink beneath the sands.

Our heroes rescue Evy and find the Book of Amun-Ra. Rick fights Imhotep long enough for the Carnahans to open the book and read the spell that makes Imhotep mortal so Rick can kill him.

Rick and the rest of the party race against the sinking city to escape but are unable to rescue Beni who is trapped surrounded by scarabs. Our heroes leave the city riding on the camels that Beni had loaded with treasure.

Past Lives:

Lord and Lady Carnahan were the patrons of the Museum of Antiquities. He was an explorer and married an Egyptian woman, who was quite an adventurer herself.

Rick's Foreign Legion garrison deserted and marched from Libya to Egypt.

Where in the World: Cairo and Hamunaptra in Egypt.

Bestiary: Mummies, lots of Mummies. Scarab beetles.

Reliquary: The Book of the Dead, the golden Book of Amun-Ra, and the puzzle box key.

No Harm Ever Came from Reading a Book:

The novelization states that the battle of Hamunaptra took place in 1925, with the rest of the movie taking place a month and two days later.

The story is expanded such as that Rick was to be hung for deserting the Legion and that Howard Carnahan was present at the opening of the tomb of Tutankhamen.

In light of revelations from The Mummy Returns, it is interesting that Evy is described as having a "Nefertiti-like shapeliness lost in a long cream linen skirt"

The Mummy Scrapbook: Also dates the events to 1925.

The Mummy: A Junior Novelization: Retells the story of the movie but sets it in 1925, however the back cover tells us that it is 1919.

The Mummy Penguin Reader: A simplified retelling of the movie based on the Junior Novelization. The jail scene is replaced with visiting Rick in the bar where Jonathan stole the key the night before and the warden is removed from the story completely. The Medjai attack on the boat is also omitted and the Carnahan siblings meet up with Rick and the American expedition at Hamunaptra.

The Mummy Annual 2003: Published in 2002, to tie into the Animated series, it opens with "The Story So Far" and gives a quick summary of *The Mummy* (1999) and again sets the movie in 1925.

Take That Bembridge Scholars!

As a remake/reboot of the 1931 Boris Karloff movie it uses the names of Imhotep and Ardeth Bay/Ardath Bey but reinvents everything else.

In this movie, Seti I is shown to killed in 1290BC, but the historical Seti I reigned from 1290BC until his death in 1279BC.

Notes

Despite his prominent role Oded Fehr's character of Ardeth Bay is not named in the movie until the end credits, although he is named in his first appearance in the novelization.

Brendan Fraser was nearly hung for real during his hanging scene.

Tom Cruise who played Nick Morton in the 2017 remake of The Mummy was a leading contender for the role of Rick O'Connell.

The Mummy Returns

The Mummy Returns (2001)*]*

Release Date: May 10, 2001

The Cast:

Brendan Fraser ....Rick O'Connell

Rachel Weisz ....Evelyn Carnahan

John Hannah ....Jonathan Carnahan

Arnold Vosloo ....Imhotep

Oded Fehr ....Ardeth Bay

Patricia Velasquez ....Anck-Su-Namun/Meela

Freddie Boath ....Alex O'Connell

Alun Armstrong ....Mr. Hafez, the Curator

Dwayne "The Rock" Johnson .....The Scorpion King

Adewale Akinnuoye-Agbaje ....Lock-Nah

Shaun Parkes ....Izzy

Bruce Byron ....Red

Joe Dixon ....Jacques

Tom Fisher ....Spivey

Aharon Ipale ....Pharaoh Seti I

Writer/Director: Stephen Sommers

Don't I know you?:

Dwayne "The Rock" Johnson – in his debut acting performance, this WWE performer has gone on to become one of the biggest names in Hollywood appearing in multiple movies including *The Fast and The Furious* franchise, *Journey 2: The Mysterious Island* (2012) (a sequel to Brendan Fraser's *Journey to the Centre of the Earth* (2008)), *Jungle Cruise* (2021), *The Rundown* (2003) (also known as *Welcome to the Jungle*), *Jumanji: Welcome to the Jungle* (2017) and *Jumanji: The Next Level* (2019).

Freddie Boath – Reportedly Boath passed on an audition in *Harry Potter and the Sorcerer's Stone (Harry Potter and the Philosopher's Stone)* (2001)

for this movie. He also appeared in *The Pillars of the Earth* (2010) and *The House of Anubis* (2013).

Alun Armstrong – In a career dating back to the 1960s, Armstrong has been consistently working including roles in *The Saint* (1997), *Van Helsing* (2004) and *Penny Dreadful* (2014).

Adewale Akinnuoye-Agbaje- This British actor also appeared in *G.I. Joe: The Rise of Cobra* (2009) as well as *Thor: The Dark World* (2013) and *Suicide Squad* (2016).

Historical Backstory:

3067 BC Thebes, 5000 years ago, a great warrior The Scorpion King led an army to conquer the known world. After seven years, the army defeated and driven into the desert of Ahm Shere. All died in the heat, until only the Scorpion King was left. He promised Anubis if his life was spared, and he could conquer his enemies, he would give Anubis his soul. The dark god agreed to the offer and spared the Scorpion King's life, creating an oasis. Anubis then gave the Scorpion King control of an army of jackal headed warriors, which soon conquered all the Scorpion King's enemies. Once the Scorpion King gained victory, the Anubis warriors returned to sand and the Scorpion King lost his soul, doomed to served Anubis for all time.

Plot Summary:

1933 Evy and Rick along with their son Alex are exploring a temple in Thebes. Alex has seen a cartouche that is the same as the tattoo on his father's wrist. Evy has been having dreams and they have led her to a secret room.

Alex sees three tomb raiders, Red, Jacques and Spivey, who are searching for something and hoping to do harm to the O'Connells. Red enters the tomb leaving his men to search the artefacts in the temple entrance. Alex distracts the men by shooting at them with his slingshot.

Rick and Evy have found the Bracelet of Anubis and evidence of the Scorpion King, but they set off a booby trap that floods the temple.

Just as his men are about to capture Alex, Red, fleeing the waters, tells them to get out. Alex accidentally knocks over several pillars that smashes a wall releasing the flood waters as well as a trapped Rick and Evy.

In Hamunaptra, there is a new dig with the Curator, Lock-Nar and Meena and the red clad cult, they have the Book of the Dead and the Book of Amun-Ra. The dig has found the new resting place of Imhotep just as Red, and his men arrive to tell them that they didn't get the bracelet but the O'Connells have taken it to London. The Curator gives Red and his men a new job as the cult is going to London to retrieve the Bracelet. Little do they know that Ardeth Bay is amongst the diggers.

The O'Connells have just gotten home and are preparing to leave to find the Oasis of Ahm Shere. Rick points out that Evy's dreams started six weeks ago with the Egyptian new year (19 July) - the Year of the Scorpion and that they should be careful. Alex has brought in the box his parents discovered and puts on the Bracelet and is given a vision of the pyramids and temple at Karnak.

Evy and Rick discover that Jonathan has been using their house while the family has been away. The cult capture Jonathan, thinking he is Rick, and discover that he has the Scepter of Osiris, which was part of the treasure the O'Connells found at the end of *The Mummy*.

Ardeth Bay arrives and there is a battle as the steal the box that had the bracelet and kidnap Evy. They follow the cult to the British Museum, where the Curator works.

Ardeth Bay tells them that they have seven days until the Scorpion King awakens and if he is killed the victor can either send back the army of Anubis or control them to take over the world. Ardeth sees Rick's tattoo and tells him that he is a Medjai.

The cult awakens Imhotep and reveal that Meela is the reincarnation of Anck-Su-Namun. Rick rescues Evy while Ardeth lays down cover fire. Imhotep calls forth four mummies.

Jonathan breaks the key to the car and hijacks a double decker bus. The O'Connells and Ardeth fight the mummies on the bus through the streets of London. Just as they stop Lock-Nar kidnaps Alex and drives off as London Bridge opened leaving his parents unable to follow. The cult won't hurt Alex until they reach the Oasis, and our heroes must race to Karnak to follow the path the bracelet shows them.

The cult is on a train to Karnak, where Imhotep meets Alex, and we discover that Red's mission was to steal the box with the Canopic jars which was discovered during the events of the Mummy. They had to kill two guards and demand more money. Meela takes them to Imhotep and tricks them into opening the chest. The Mummy then restores himself by sucking them dry

In Cairo, Rick visits his friend and pilot Izzy to fly them to Karnak. Izzy complains that he is always getting shot when he is with Rick. He agrees to help in return for the Scepter of Osiris and they fly off in his dirigible. The tribes of the Medjai are following on horseback to battle the army of Anubis if needed.

Alex tries to escape just as they reach Karnak, the Bracelet gives him a vision of the next location, and he is recaptured. Imhotep shows Meela several of her memories of her time as Anck-Su-Namun and restores her soul. This spell also brings out memories of a past life for Evy revealing that she was Nefertiri, daughter of Seti I.

Alex has been leaving clues in their journey for his parents to follow. Following the Blue Nile, Lock-Nar discovers this, and Imhotep sends a wall of water after the O'Connell party. Izzy fires his jet engines but runs out of gas just as they reach Ahm Shere, and they crash. Izzy works to repair his damaged vehicle as Ardeth sends Horus, his hawk to summon the other Medjai but Lock-Nar shoots the bird.

Both Imhotep and the O'Connell parties enter the jungle surrounding the Oasis and are attacked by the pygmy mummies that live there. Rick rescues Alex and after defeating Lock-Nar, Ardeth goes to get the rest of the Medjai. Father and son race the sun to the temple, just making it before the sun hits. The bracelet falls off Alex's wrist saving his life.

Just as Evy and Jonathan arrive, Anck-Su-Namun stabs Evy and kills her.

Imhotep and Anck-Su-Namun enter the temple and Imhotep is stripped of his powers. The Curator finds the Bracelet of Anubis and activates the temple awaking the Scorpion King and the Anubis army, just as the Medjai arrive. Jonathan and Alex retrieve the Book of the Dead and resurrect Evy, as Rick heads into the temple to kill Imhotep.

Outside the Medjai battle the Army of Anubis. Rick finds Imhotep and the pair battle, only to be interrupted by the arrival of the Scorpion King, who is revealed to be a half human, half giant scorpion creature. Imhotep swears loyalty to the Scorpion King, and the beast attacks Rick before killing the Curator. The Medjai defeat the first wave of Anubis warriors.

Rick discovers that the scepter opens into a spear and uses it to kill the Scorpion King and send the army of Anubis back to the underworld. Both Rick and Imhotep are grabbed by the souls of the underworld, where Evy helps Rick, Anck-Su-Namun flees, and Imhotep falls to his death in the underworld. Anck-Su-Namun falls into a pit of scarabs.

As the whole oasis and surrounding jungle are being sucked into the Underworld; the O'Connell party is rescued by Izzy in his repaired balloon. Jonathan steals the diamond from the top of the pyramid as the balloon takes off.

Past Lives:

Literally, we discover that Evy is the reincarnation of Nefertiri, daughter of Seti I.

Alex states that he is eight.

Rick got his tattoo at an orphanage in Cairo.

Rick and Izzy did a bank job in Marrakesh where Izzy got shot and Rick ran off with a belly dancer girl. Rick and Izzy also went surfing in Tripoli.

Jonathan is a three-time fox and hounds' champion.

Where in the World: London, Egypt, and the Oasis of Ahm Shere.

Bestiary: Mummies, pygmy mummies, and the half man–half scorpion that is The Scorpion King.

Reliquary: The Bracelet of Anubis, the Scepter of Osiris.

No Harm Ever Came From Reading a Book:

The Mummy Annual 2003: Published in 2002, to tie into the Animated series, it opens with "The Story So Far" and gives a quick summary of *The Mummy Returns* (2001) and sets the movie in 1935.

The novelization by Max Allan Collins: Instead of 3067BC, The Scorpion King's campaign took place in 3112BC and lasted five years instead of seven. Rick is a Knight Templar, not a Medjai,, and he got his tattoo in an orphanage in Hong Kong instead of Egypt. Izzy and Rick went on an adventure two years ago (1931), which caused Izzy to be shot in the ass. To show devotion to the Scorpion King, adherents must scalp themselves as the Scorpion King had been, in the final battle both Imhotep and the Curator scalp themselves.

The Mummy Returns Scrapbook: Retells the movie from Alex's perspective. No date is given but his parents met ten years ago. The Scorpion King's original campaign was in 4000BC. The Curator is removed from the story. Rick is a Masonic Templar.

The Mummy Returns Junior Novelization: The Scorpion King had been scalped. Rick and Evy met ten years ago. The Scorpion King was active 6 thousand years ago. Rick is a Masonic Templar and got the tattoo in Hong Kong.

The Mummy Returns Penguin Reader: Dates the Scorpion King's original campaign to 4000BC and that he had been inactive for 6 thousand years before being awoken in 1933. It says that Rick and Evy met ten years earlier (1923). The story is simplified and removes the character of the Curator. Rick is referred to as a Masonic Templar. The Scepter of Osiris doesn't appear, Rick finds the painting of the Osiris (which gave the instructions on how to use the spear in the movie) and gives a Masonic passphrase which magically gives him a sword. Jonathan never gets the giant diamond at the top of the pyramid.

Take That Bembridge Scholars!

Seti I's son, Ramesses II was married to a woman named Nefertari and had a daughter of the same name. There is no record of a daughter named Nefertiri.

In *The Ten Commandments* (1956) Seti is referred to as Sethi (Sir Cedric Hardwick) and his future daughter-in-law Princess Nefretiri (Anne Baxter).

Notes:

Red says that the Yanks who found the box 9 years ago came to a bad end. Nine years before 1933 would be 1924 – instead of 1926 when the first movie was set – although math may not be Red's strong suit.

The train has a shrine with the five Canopic jars from the Mummy, but in that movie one of them was broken and all five are whole here.

The glass panels of the train have an image of a phoenix, which Alex would later encounter in "The Flight of the Phoenix."

With the Egyptian New Year being July 19, and Rick stating that was 6 weeks ago, most of the movie takes place in late August/early September 1933.

The Mummy: Tomb of the Dragon Emperor

The Mummy: Tomb of the Dragon Emperor (2008)

Release Date: September 11, 2008

The Cast:

Brendan Fraser ....Rick O'Connell

Maria Bello............................Evelyn Carnahan

John Hannah ....Jonathan Carnahan

Jet Li ....The Emperor

Michelle Yeoh ....Zi Yuan

Luke Ford ....Alex O'Connell

Isabella Leong ....Lin

Liam Cunningham ....Mad Dog Maguire

Anthony Chau–Sang Wong ...General Yang

David Calder ....Roger Wilson

Writers: Alfred Gough and Miles Millar

Director: Rob Cohen

Don't I know you?:

Rob Cohen: The director of *Dragonheart* (1996), *The Fast and the Furious* (2001), *xXx* (2002) and *Alex Cross* (2012).

Alfred Gough and Miles Millar: This writing team wrote *Lethal Weapon 4* (1998), *Spider-Man 2* (2004), and created *Smallville* (2001-2011).

Jet Li: This Chinese actor appeared in a number of Hong Kong films including *Black Mask* (1996) and *The Once Upon a Time in China* series as well as Western movies *Lethal Weapon 4* and *The Expendables* series as well as playing the Emperor of China in *Mulan* (2020).

Michelle Yeoh: Appeared in many Hong Kong movies including the *Heroic Trio* series, *Silver Hawk* (2004) as well as Western productions *Tomorrow Never Dies* (1997), *Star Trek: Discovery* (2017- present) and *Shang Chi and the Legend of the Ten Rings* (2021).

Maria Bello: appeared in TV series *Mr. & Mrs. Smith* (1996–1997), *ER* (1997–1998), the American version of *Prime Suspect* (2011–2012) and *NCIS* (2017–2021) as well as movies such as *A History of Violence* (2005), *Coyote Ugly* (2000) and *The Jane Austen Book Club* (2007).

Luke Ford: This Australian actor appeared in a number of Australian productions including *Home and Away* (2000) and *Cleverman* (2017)

Historical Backstory:

During a civil war in ancient China, one king wanted rule it all. Assassins tried to kill him but failed, and he destroyed all opposition and became known as the Dragon Emperor. He enslaved his defeated enemies to build the Great Wall.

He was trained by his mystics to control the five elements. He sought immortality and sent his general Ming to find a witch Zi Yuan, rumored to know the secret.

Zi Yuan and General Ming were sent to the monastery at Turfan to search their library. They discovered the Oracle Bones, a collection of ancient wisdom.

Using the book, she cast a spell in Sanskrit however the spell has a curse and the Emperor, and his men are turned to terracotta. Zi Yuan rides away

Plot Summary:

Rick is fishing and returns home to find that Evy is out. He stares at his old Legionnaire uniform longing for the past. Evy is at a book signing of her two novels, *The Mummy* and *The Mummy Returns,* she has written based on their adventures. Evy has writer's block for her third novel.

The couple later meet for dinner, and they are bored as they retired from adventuring after the Second World War. Alex is supposed to be at college.

Alex is actually on a dig in China with Professor Roger Wilson. At college, he found a Bembridge Journal that led him to the site. They blast open the tomb and find the body of Sir Colin Bembridge, who searched for the tomb 70 years ago. They set off several booby traps, losing two of their party, before discovering the terracotta army.

Alex and Wilson explore the tomb and find a Feng Shui compass. After solving the riddle of the compass, they find the body of the Dragon Emperor. Alex and the professor are attacked black clad martial artist. Alex discovers that their attacker is a young woman who promptly escapes.

Rick and Evy are visited by British Intelligence, thanking them for them for their service in World War Two and offers them one last mission to deliver the Eye of Shangri-La to the museum in Shanghai. They accept the mission to visit as an opportunity to visit Jonathan in Shanghai.

Jonathan owns an Egyptian themed nightclub named Imhoteps. Alex is celebrating at his uncle's club on Chinese New Year when Rick and Evy walk in. Alex gets in a fight with Maddog Maguire, who served with Rick in the Legionnaires, over a woman. The family reunion doesn't go well and Rick and Evy try to work out how to repair their relationship with Alex.

The next night Rick and Evy visit the Museum to see the Emperor's mummy. The Emperor's coffin is on a carriage pulled by four bronze horses. Professor Wilson sees the O'Connells to retrieve the Eye of Shangri-La. It is a double cross as General Yang arrives and threatens Rick and Evy to unlock the Eye of Shangri-La.

Alex discovers the girl who attacked him in the tomb is there and her name is Lin and finds out that she is trying to prevent the Emperor from being awakened. General Yang, who wishes to resurrect the Emperor to rule China, discovers that the blood of the pure of heart will activate the Eye. The Eye contains waters from the Pool of Eternal Life that will awaken the Emperor.

Alex and Lin swing into action to prevent the Emperor's resurrection but are unsuccessful. The newly resurrected Emperor brings his bronze horses to life. The Emperor brad the general race out of the Museum into the streets with Alex and Lin underneath. Evy and Rick highjack a fireworks truck to chase the Emperor Mummy.

A chase through the streets of Shanghai ensues, ending with the Emperor escaping and the truck exploding. The O'Connell family and Lin regroup at Imhoteps. Lin tells them that the Emperor will head for

Shangri-La, and they follow, Maddog Maguire flies them in and lands them halfway up the mountain.

General Yang introduces the Emperor to the modern world and uses the Eye of Shangri-La to guide them to the Pool of Eternal Life.

The O'Connells and Lin make it to the Gates of Shangri-La and wire the Golden Temple to explode and attack the troops as they arrive. The battle doesn't go well, and Lin calls for three yetis. The yetis throw the soldiers around as Jonathan lights the explosives.

The Emperor arrives chases off the Yeti and extinguishes the explosives and places the diamond at the top of the temple which shows him the way to Shangri-La. The Emperor throws his sword at Alex, but Rick takes the blade.

They take a dying Rick to Shangri-La and Zi Yuan heals Rick with the water of the Pool of Eternal Life. Lin and Zi Yuan explain to Alex that they had been alive for over two thousand years guarding the Emperor.

The Emperor bathes in the pool becoming immortal. He transforms into a three headed dragon and kidnaps Lin and returns to his tomb.

The O'Connells and Zi Yuan race back to Maddog who drops them at the tomb. Zi Yuan sacrifices her and Lin's immortality to call for the spirits of the dead in the Great Wall as an army to battle the revived terracotta army who must cross the wall to become immortal.

There is a battle of the undead. Zi Yuan battles the Emperor and sacrifices herself to retrieve the dagger, the only weapon that can kill him.

The Emperor becomes a Nian (also known as Fu dog) attacking the undead army.

Lin gets the dagger from her mother just before she dies. The O'Connells battle the Emperor, but the dagger is broken. They drive both parts of the blade into his heart killing the Emperor and causing the terracotta army to fall. Their job done the wall spirits return to dust.

Maddog takes over Imhoteps as Jonathan leaves with the Eye of Shangri-La for somewhere without mummies like Peru. The caption tells us that "soon after mummies were found in Peru."

Past Lives:

Rick and Evy worked for British Intelligence during World War II. Alex was studying at Harvard.

Where in the World: China and England

Bestiary: The Emperor turns into a three headed dragon and a giant Nian, terracotta soldiers and undead warriors buried in Great Wall of China and the Yeti.

Reliquary: The Oracle Bones, The Eye of Shangri-La, the Pool of Eternal Life, the Dragon Knife.

No Harm Ever Came From Reading a Book:

The novelization by Max Allan Collins: At age 14 during World War Two, Alex was sent to Australia for the duration of the war.

The Helbling Reader: a simplified retelling of the movie.

Notes:

Rachel Weisz elected not to return citing issues with the script. Both Maria Bello and Luke Ford had three picture contracts.

In the novelization of *The Scorpion King* by Max Allan Collins, it is revealed that the fur Mathayus is wearing in the opening scene comes from a yeti.

The Mummy: The Animated Series

The Mummy: The Complete Series DVD (2001–2003)

Regular Cast

> Alex O'Connell............Chris Marquette
>
> Rick O'Connell...........John Schneider
>
> Evy O'Connell............Grey Griffin (as Grey DeLisle)
>
> Jonathan Carnahan.....Tom Kenny
>
> Ardeth Bay................Nicholas Guest
>
> Colin Weasler............Michael Reisz
>
> Imhotep...................Jim Cummings

Don't I Know You:

Chris Marquette – began his career at the age of four and has appeared in *Fillmore! (2002-2004)*, *Joan of Arcadia (2003-2005)*, and *Barry (2018-current)*.

John Schneider: Most famous as Bo Duke in *The Dukes of Hazzard (1979-1985)*, Schneider also appeared as Jonathan Kent in *Smallville* (2001-2011), and his one-time character of Dallas Carter in *Relic Hunter* (1999-2002) may have been the model for his portrayal as Rick O'Connell.

Grey Griffin: Credited for many years under her married name Grey DeLisle, this actress added her voice to numerous cartoons including various installments of the *Scooby Doo* franchise, *The Grim Adventures of Billy and Mandy (2001-2007)*, and *Clifford the Big Red Dog* (2000–2003) as well as many DC and Marvel characters.

Jim Cummings: the voice of Winnie the Pooh and Tigger in the *Winnie The Pooh* franchise, as well as providing voices for the animated series *Darkwing Duck (1991-1992)*, *Captain Planet and the Planeteers (1990-1996)*, and *Taz-Mania (1991-1995)*.

1-1 "The Summoning"

Release Date: September 29, 2001

The Cast:

Alex O'Connell

Rick O'Connell

Evy O'Connell

Jonathan Carnahan

Ardeth Bay

Colin Weasler

Imhotep

Guest Cast

Sir Arthur Fenwick………Nicholas Guest

Writer: Tom Pugsley and Greg Klein.

Director: Eddie Houchins

Historical Backstory:

In the opening, Imhotep tries to steal the Manacle of Osiris and the Scrolls of Thebes and is punished with mummification.

Plot Summary

On vacation in Scotland, the O'Connells visit a 12th century castle and discover a Moorish bowl. Alex opens a door releasing a flock of bats and loosening the masonry causing a collapse. When Evy takes the bowl to the British Museum Sof Antiquities, the curator, Sir Arthur Fenwick, makes her the Chief Archaeologist in recognition of her discovery of the Book of the Dead. Colin Weasler, who believed that he should have got the job is upset and storms off.

The O'Connells head to the airfield the next day to fly in a Zephyr to the dig in Hamunaptra and Jonathan joins them avoid an angry creditor.

Alex is unhappy to discover that he will be home-schooled during this trip.

At the dig, Jonathan falls through the floor and discovers the Temple of Bort* (see notes). The O'Connells then find the Manacle of Osiris, a bracelet forged by Osiris to vanquish his foes.

Meanwhile, Colin Weasler had stolen the Book of the Dead from the British Museum and travelled to Egypt where he resurrected Imhotep. Imhotep is buried in a temple near Hamunaptra and is bandaged. Instead of obeying Weasler's commands, Imhotep steals the book and uses it to return to his human form and to resurrect several other mummies.

Later at the camp, Alex puts on the Manacle and gains visions of the future where he is tied to an altar and Imhotep is attacking him.

Shortly after Weasler and Imhotep attack the O'Connells, but Ardeth Bay comes to their defense. Imhotep forms a whirlwind and kidnaps Alex. Ardeth explains that Alex won't be harmed until Imhotep gains the Scrolls of Thebes, which are rumored to be buried with King Djoser in his pyramid in Saqqara.

Imhotep drops Weasler and Alex at the pyramid and opens a doorway before seeing the Zephyr. He pulls out a scarab stone, which he turns into a large scarab and sends towards the Zephyr. The Zephyr is infiltrated by a hoard of black scarabs. Evy and Rick drive out the scarabs, with Rick using his butt to block a hole in the balloon.

The O'Connells confront Imhotep, who awakens several soldier mummies. Alex cries out in fear, and the Manacle glows and emits a beam destroying the mummies. Evy finds the Book of the Dead and begins to read the spell to destroy Imhotep. She is tackled by Weasler mid spell and Imhotep is left weakened and undead. The Book of the Dead falls down a crevice and is lost.

Past Lives:

There are references to the events of *The Mummy* and *The Mummy Returns*

Where in the World: Scotland in 12th Century castle, London at the British Museum of Antiquities. Hamunaptra and Saqqara in Egypt.

Bestiary: Imhotep, soldier mummies, black scarabs.

Reliquary: The Book of the Dead, the Manacle of Osiris, the Scarab stone.

No Harm Ever Came from Reading a Book:

The Mummy Annual follows the plot of the episode closely except it states that Alex's age is eleven which is not given in the episode. The annual also gives the name of the Curator of the British Museum of Antiquities as Sir Arthur Fenwick. At the end of "The Story so Far..," we are told that this series takes place in 1938.

Take That Bembridge Scholars!:

Rather than the doomed love story of resurrecting Anck-Su-Namun, Imhotep is trying to steal the manacle of Osiris and the Scrolls of Thebes.

Notes:

Alex mentions Olympic bobsledding which suggests that he may have been recently listening to the 1936 Berlin Winter Games, where the US won Gold and Bronze in the two-man bobsled, and the UK won Bronze in the four-man sled. This would align with the Spring half term explaining why Alex isn't in school. The 1936 date also matches the Alex's age of 11 as stated in the annual adaptation of this adventure.

The temple of Bort which Jonathan found, it doesn't appear that there are any deities by that name. The temple has a lion-headed statue – the deity depicted with a lion head and the closest name is Bast.

You would think that after the events of *The Mummy Returns*, that Alex would know better than to play around with ancient Egyptian relics, having said that you could say the same for Evy and Rick.

No explanation as to how Imhotep was moved to a tomb for Weasler to resurrect him after his death in *The Mummy Returns*, at the Oasis of

Ahm Shere. However, given that Ardeth Bay was aware of the attack on the guards it seems likely that the Medjai were involved.

The Djoser Step Pyramid was built for the burial of King Djoser by the historical Imhotep in the 27th Century BC. Imhotep was deified after his death and presumably Imhotep from 1290BC was named after this Imhotep.

1-2 "A Candle in the Darkness"

Release Date: October 6, 2001

The Cast:

Alex O'Connell

Rick O'Connell

Evy O'Connell

Jonathan Carnahan

Colin Weasler

Imhotep

Writer Steven Melching

Director Eddie Houchins

Plot Summary

The family has looked for the Scrolls of Thebes, all over Alexandria, the last known location of the scrolls. Alex is unhappy that he must be home-schooled and ditches his homework to go into town with his uncle. Weasler has just arrived and reports to Imhotep that he found the O'Connells.

There is an earthquake that opens a secret chamber of the Library of Alexandria. Alex has a vision of a light in the darkness. Alex and Jonathan explore the chamber and find a map room. Alex draws it but they are discovered by Weasler and Imhotep. Imhotep makes a sand wall with his face to chase Alex and Jonathan on his sidecar motorcycle. Jonathan uses the water from the river to stop Imhotep.

When Alex returns, Evy discovers that the map shows an annex to the main library. The family heads to explore the annex and finds the library's index scrolls but are discovered by Imhotep who reads from a scroll and sends shadow demons to attack the family. Evy burns the index scroll after memorizing the contents.

Alex falls into a trap and his father goes to rescue him, as Evy and Jonathan try to find the scrolls.

The family reunites and uses the mirrors lighting to destroy the shadow demons and Alex uses the manacle to call the scrolls and books to attack Imhotep, who flees.

Evy grabs a slip of paper saying that Alexander the Great borrowed the scrolls. The family must find Alexander's diary

Past Lives:

Jonathan would prefer to dance the Charleston.

Where in the World: Alexandria, Egypt.

Bestiary: Shadow demons.

Reliquary: The index scrolls, the map room.

No Harm Ever Came From Reading a Book:

The Mummy Annual no changes to the plot of the episode or new information.

Notes:

Alexander the Great (356BC–323BC) founded the city of Alexandria in 331BC. It is unclear if the original Scrolls or copies were held in the library annex. It seems that he would have borrowed the scrolls between 331BC when the city was founded and 326BC when he left for India. The actual Library at Alexandria was not built until a century later, so it appears that the Annex that the O'Connells found was a precursor to the main Library.

1-3 "Against The Elements"

The Mummy "Against the Elements" Reader

Release Date: October 13, 2001

The Cast:

Alex O'Connell

Rick O'Connell

Evy O'Connell

Jonathan Carnahan

Ardeth Bay

Colin Weasler

Imhotep

Guest cast

Salah, Sherpa guide and a spy for Weasler no dialog.

Writer: Tom Pugsley and Greg Klein.

Director: Eddie Houchins

Plot Summary:

The O'Connells are in India where they find the diary of Alexander the Great, but Jonathan steals the jewel from the forehead of a statue of Buddha activating the temple's booby traps (sinking ceiling and blow darts from the wall). Alex uses the diary to save his uncle destroying it in the process. However, he did save the page saying the scrolls were left at the palace of Merneptah in Memphis.

The Zephyr is out of commission and the O'Connells must arrange alternate transport. While waiting Alex and Jonathan see a snake charmer, Jonathan upsets the cobra. They are rescued by a mongoose, which Alex adopts and names Tut. He doesn't tell his parents, but Rick is allergic to Tut and sneezes whenever the animal is around.

The family rides elephants from India. They arrive in Egypt and then sail the Nile in a boat.

Imhotep finds the Staff of Set, which controls the elements summoning a water dragon who attacks their boat. Ardeth Bay rescues the O'Connells. At camp they discuss that Imhotep is on the move and has the Staff to bolster his powers.

The O'Connells find the palace buried in the sand and blast it out. Imhotep appears and brings to life the two guardian statues and kidnaps Alex. Rick and Evy follow Alex leaving Jonathan and Ardeth to fight the stone mummies.

Imhotep summons a wind demon to attack Rick and Evy. Alex uses two belts to rescue his parents before the manacle destroys the demon.

Jonathan and Ardeth blow up the stone guardians with dynamite.

Imhotep then unleashes two fire hounds to distract the O'Connells while he searches for the scrolls. The box he finds is empty. Tut attacks Imhotep while Alex steals the Staff of Set and uses the staff to stop the fire hounds and set them against Imhotep. Imhotep turns to sand and disappears. Alex then breaks the staff causing the hounds to vanish.

The O'Connells vow to follow Alexander's footsteps to find the scrolls.

Past Lives:

Alex had a pet lizard that got loose in a museum.

Where in the World: India, Memphis, Egypt.

Bestiary: A Water dragon, stone guardians, wind demons, and fire hounds.

Reliquary: The Diary of Alexander the Great (destroyed), The Staff of Set (broken).

No Harm Ever Came From Reading a Book:

Annual: no changes to the plot of the episode or new information.

Penguin reader: The story conflates the events of "the Summoning" with this adventure and the discovery of the manacle at the same time as the Diary of Alexander. It describes the trip from India to Memphis as taking three days and that the water dragon has Imhotep's face. They also spell Ardeth Bay's name as Ardeth Bey.

At the back of the book there are three chants that relate to the events of the adventure.

Notes:

Presumably, the O'Connells only rode the elephants to the nearest airport as overland the trip would likely have taken months.

1-4 "The Deep Blue Sea"

Release Date: 20 October 2001

The Cast:

Alex O'Connell

Rick O'Connell

Evy O'Connell

Imhotep

Guest Cast:

Dimitri Helios...........John Kassir

Writer Tony Schillaci

Director Eddie Houchins

Don't I know you?:

John Kassir provided the voice of the Crypt Keeper in the *Tales of the Crypt* franchise.

Historical Backstory:

The Scrolls of Thebes were on a ship named the Athena which unloaded in Minosos which sunk around 400BC from the fist of Zeus.

Plot Summary:

The O'Connells have found stone tablets describing the voyage of the Athena when Imhotep attacks breaking the tablets. The manacle drives the mummy away and Evy grabs a couple of pieces. Alex touches one and gets a vision showing him the location of Minosos, off the coast of Crete.

Evy knows of a submarine captained by Dimitri Helios. They set sail but Imhotep, in the form of a water funnel, attacks the submarine. At 10000 fathoms, the pressure is too much for Imhotep but the submarine crashes on the bottom of the ocean.

Dimitri has three scuba tanks and diving suits, Alex and Dimitri repair the submarine and Rick visits Minosos,

Imhotep summons and controls a sea creature who attacks the repair crew and follows Rick to the city. Rick has found the log, but it is booby trapped. The monster attacks and Rick uses the booby trap to trap the monster and grab the logbooks.

Evy begins translating the logbooks but does not reveal what they said.

Where in the World: Greece.

Bestiary: The sea monster. Zeus is mentioned.

Reliquary: The Athena's logbook.

Notes:

While the acronym SCUBA (Self-Contained Underwater Breathing Apparatus), was not coined until the innovations of Jacques Costeau in the 1940s and Christian Lambertson in the 1950s, closed circuit diving suits had been invented in 1926 by Yves Le Prier and Maurice Fernez. This was likely the type of suit used by Helios.

Helios' submarine was likely a surplus submarine from The Great War (World War One 1914-1918).

1-5 "Eruption"

Release Date: 27 October 2001

The Cast:

Alex O'Connell

Rick O'Connell

Evy O'Connell

Jonathan Carnahan

Guest cast

Ishi…………..Dionne Quan

Chief………Amy Hill

Writer: Tom Pugsley and Greg Klein.

Director: Eddie Houchins

Don't I know you?:

Amy Hill: Amy provided voices for *Lilo and Stich* (movie and series) as well as playing Kumo in the reboot of *Magnum P.I.* (2018).

Plot Summary

In a Turkish mine shaft, the O'Connells and Jonathan have found a book but are pursued in mine carts by Imhotep and a two headed mummy monster with jackal heads. After dispatching the two headed mummy, Imhotep is knocked out. There is a break in the tracks but Rick with his whip rescues the family.

Once they exit the mine, Evy reveals that they have found the naval records of Lord Haverford, the mine's owner. Haverford served under Captain James Cook when he founded a new English colony Australia.

As the zephyr flies, Alex has a vision and nearly sleepwalks off the ship. The zephyr is struck by lightning and must put down for repairs. The emergency landing has broken a statue.

Alex and Evy search for food and water and get stuck in quicksand but are rescued by Ishi, a local girl. Ishi's mother is the chief and offers to help repair the zephyr.

Alex shows off his remote-controlled plane and Ishi throws a boomerang. The pair hangout tightrope walking and surfing.

The broken statue awakens a lava creature, the te'ma'kauwai, who controls the local volcano, which is threatening to erupt. The O'Connells offer to help and make a plan. The chief mentions the legend of a firewalker who may appease the creature.

Ishi attempts to cross the lava and is rescued by Alex. Rick at the same time uses the fire extinguisher to defeat the creature. The statue is rebuilt and the O'Connells promise to return.

Where in the World: Turkey, unnamed Pacific Island.

Bestiary: The te'ma'kauwai.

Notes:

Captain Cook was not the founder the colony of Australia. In 1768, Captain James Cook sailed from England with orders to view the transit of Venus from Tahiti. He then opened secret orders to search for Terra Australis, the unknown southern land. He explored many of the Pacific islands including New Zealand and was the first European to discover and map the east coast of Australia, naming it New South Wales in 1770. Cook made to further journeys exploring the Pacific and died in 1779 in an altercation in Hawaii.

It was not until 1786 was it decided to colonize New South Wales with a fleet of ships lead by Captain Arthur Phillip who was the first Governor landing in 1788. The nation of Australia was formed on January 1, 1900. However, it was Cook's voyages that lead to the settlement of New South Wales and the eventual creation of Australia. It appears that Evy was simplifying somewhat.

It is unclear where the island is located presumably somewhere in Melanesia with evidence that they were trading with both Australian

First Nations people (as evidenced by the boomerang) and Polynesian Islanders (the surfboard).

It is likely that the Zephyr was following Cook's path to Tahiti before exploring the Pacific and the mapping of the east coast of what is now Australia.

1-6 "The Orb of Aten"

Release Date: November 3, 2001

The Cast:

Alex O'Connell

Rick O'Connell

Evy O'Connell

Imhotep

Colin Weasler

Guest Cast

Babe Ruth……………Maurice LaMarche

Writer: Nick Dubois

Director: Eddie Houchins

Don't I know you?:

Maurice LaMarche, the voice of Yosemite Sam in *Looney Tunes* and the Brain in *Animaniacs* and the spinoffs *Pinky and the Brain*, and *Pinky, Elmyra and the Brain*.

Historical Backstory:

The Orb of Aten was broken in two and hidden by Alexander the Great's men. In 1916, an American dig discovered one half of the Orb in Biyala Egypt.

Plot Summary

The O'Connells are looking for an object of great power that Alexander had hidden in a pyramid referenced in the Logbooks of the Athena - they discover one half of Orb of Aten. Imhotep steals the orb and throws the O'Connells out of the pyramid. They use a tarp as parachute to survive the fall.

The O'Connells realize that Imhotep is seeking the other half of the Orb. Evy recalls it being discovered in a dig in 1916 and contacts Fenwick, the curator of the British Museum of Antiquities to see where it is currently located.

They are advised that the orb is on loan to the Museum of Ancient History in New York City. The O'Connells take off in the zephyr. Weasler, has been spying on Fenwick's communications with the O'Connells is aware of the orb's location and he has booked passage on a ship for himself and Imhotep to New York. The O'Connells arrive first and take in the sights (Coney Island and a carriage ride in Central Park) before the Museum opens.

The Museum also holds the Book of Thoth. The curator is delayed so Alex and Rick travel to Stadium. It turns out that Rick knew Babe Ruth at the Saint Mary's Industrial School for Boys. Babe Ruth heard that Rick had joined the Foreign Legion. The O'Connells join the practice session.

Hardy, the curator, refuses to give Evy the Orb suggesting that she is crazy. The O'Connells break into the Museum to steal the Orb but Imhotep is there first and has rejoined both halves of the Orb. Imhotep summons a plague of insects and Evy decides to use the Book of Thoth to stop Imhotep. Alex stops the bugs, but Imhotep brings to life a T-Rex skeleton and leaves the Museum to perform the ritual to regain his powers. This ritual requires sunlight.

Evy reads a spell from the Book of Thoth to stop the T-Rex skeleton. They follow Imhotep to the Statue of Liberty and Evy reads a spell to create an eclipse. Weasler attacks Evy who drops the Book of Thoth into the water. Meanwhile, Rick fights with Imhotep and drops the Orb. Alex hits it with a sledgehammer and destroys the Orb.

Rick as Rick 'The Rocket" O'Connell plays in the game with Babe Ruth.

Past Lives:

Rick knew George "Babe" Ruth at St Mary's Industrial School for Boys in Baltimore.

Where in the World: Egypt and New York City.

Bestiary: Aten was a powerful Egyptian sun god.

Reliquary: The Orb of Aten, the book of Thoth.

Notes:

Jonathan is still in Greece with a head cold. It seems that this episode should follow "The Deep Blue Sea" which was set in Greece. Jonathan was not in that episode and likely came down sick just prior to the events of that episode. Jonathan is back in "Eruption."

The O'Connells are following the lead found in the logbook of the Athena as seen in "The Deep Blue Sea".

This episode officially names the curator of the British Museum as Fenwick.

The Zephyr is docked at the top of the Empire State Building. While the spire at the top was intended for the docking of airships, shortly after opening it was found to be too windy for docking with unpredictable eddies, shortly after it opened in 1931.

Babe Ruth was at the St Mary's Industrial School for Boys from 1902 until 1914. Since we later discover in "Like Father, Like Son" that Jack O'Connell left his family around 1912 it is likely that Rick met Babe Ruth at that time.

Babe Ruth left the Yankees in 1934 and retired after the 1935 season. By 1936 he was playing exhibition games, presumably the game seen at the end of the episode was one of those.

Thoth is also known as Tehuti and the Book of Thoth in this episode does bear a resemblance to the Book of Tehuti seen in *The Scorpion King: The Akkadian Prophecy*. It is unclear if the Scroll of Thoth seen in *The Mummy* (1932) is connected to the book – it may be a page from the book.

1-7 "The Black Forest"

Release Date: November 10, 2001

The Cast:

Alex O'Connell

Rick O'Connell

Evy O'Connell

Jonathan Carnahan

Imhotep

Colin Weasler

Guest Cast:

Albert Einstein..............Jim Ward

Writer: Elaine Zicree and Marc Zicree.

Director: Eddie Houchins

Historical Backstory:

Ancient Roman scholars had translated the location of the scrolls into a mathematical formula

Plot Summary:

The O'Connells and Weasler discover that there is a mathematical formula showing the scrolls' location. The tablets were hidden in a church in London, Weasler finds the tablets, but Rick tackles him, and Alex grabs the tablets. Imhotep appears and snatches Evy in his tornado and drops her on one of the hands of Big Ben.

Rick hands over the tablets but Imhotep uses his magic to throw gears at Rick to cover his escape. Rick rescues Evy and they miss Imhotep. Evy says there is only one man who can solve this equation, Albert Einstein. As they prepare to leave Jonathan arrives to join the party.

Weasler and Imhotep kidnap Einstein leaving behind some sand. Alex touches the sand and gets a vision of a castle in the Black Forest.

Imhotep is impatient and threatens Einstein. Believing that the O'Connells to be on their way, Imhotep summons the spirits of the forest, Katzenweise★. Trees come to life attacking the O'Connells dragging the adults into a tree trunk. The adults are trapped in the castle as Alex runs through the forest with trees throwing pine needles at him,

Alex finds the castle and the topiary animals come to life. Alex causes them to fight each other, and he enters the castle.

Weasler taunts the adults but Rick tricks him into allowing him to escape. Alex has freed Einstein, and they reunite. The Katzenweise attack but Alex uses the manacle which frees the spirits who attack Imhotep.

Weasler finds that Einstein has solved the problem and left the co-ordinates for Borneo on the board. Einstein reveals to the O'Connells that he left a false answer on the board and the true solution to the problem is in his head.

Alex despairs at working out how to use the manacle but Einstein says there must be a pattern and once he finds the pattern Alex can use the manacle.

Past Lives:

Evy spent a summer studying under Einstein in Germany.

Where in the World: London, Berlin, and the Black Forest in Germany.

Bestiary: Katzenweise, German forest spirits.

Reliquary: The Roman tablets.

Notes:

It sounds like Evy calls the forest spirits Katzenweise, but I was unable to locate any forest spirit of that or a similar name. Forest spirit in German in Waldgeist and Katzen is German for cat.

Jonathan mentions that the family was heading to Paris, no mention of what clue was leading them there.

Einstein never reveals the solution to the problem in this episode.

After 1933, Einstein had left Germany after the rise of Adolf Hitler and was living in America. His old house had become a Hitler Youth Camp by the time of this episode.

There is an inconsistency in this episode, it is shown that Imhotep kidnapped Einstein after a lecture, but the O'Connell's find sand in Einstein's house (supposedly in Berlin). It is possible that Einstein convinced the mummy to let him take some things from his house and that is how the sand got there. The house would most likely be in Princeton, New Jersey, where Einstein was teaching at the Institute for Advanced Study.

It may be assumed that the O'Connells escorted Einstein back to America before following the clue that the scrolls were in the Mojave desert, as revealed in the next episode.

1-8 "The Cloud People"

Release Date: November 17, 2001

The Cast:

Alex O'Connell

Rick O'Connell

Evy O'Connell

Colin Weasler

Imhotep

Guest cast:

The elder

Pilow.....................Ulysses Cuardo

Tiga.....................Candy Milo

Writer: Robert Skir and Martin Isenberg.

Director: Eddie Houchins

Plot Summary:

Following Einstein's clue, the O'Connells find themselves in the Mojave desert. Alex has a vision of nearly finding the scrolls but being attacked by Imhotep and seeing a lake shaped like a big cat.

After coming out of the vision, Alex sets off several of the booby traps in the cave. The O'Connells escape and Alex tells his parents of vision. Rick recognizes the lake as Lake Titicaca in Peru.

Meanwhile Weasler and Imhotep are exploring ruins in England tracking the scrolls after a trip to Borneo. Weasler thinks he has found the scrolls, but it is another dead end. Weasler intercepts Evy's telegram to Sir Colin Fenwick telling him of their trip to Peru.

Evy believes that Pizarro may have had the scrolls in his exploration of Peru and Rick mentions the Cloud People in Andes Mountains. Alex is feeling the pressure of always moving around unable to make friends. Imhotep has arrived and is following them up the mountain.

The O'Connells are attacked by a caroupia★, a mountain spirit. Rick defeats the creature but spares its life. The Chachapoyas or Cloud people reveal themselves to the family and assist them to the top of the mountain. Imhotep and Weasler have also been climbing the mountain.

The O'Connells are taken to the hidden city of the cloud people and for sparing the life of the Caroupia, the cloud people at their service. They offer to take them to the treasure of Pizarro but like Pizarro they must keep the existence of the Cloud people secret.

The elders take Evy and Rick to the treasure of Pizarro while Alex stays and plays with the local children. However, Imhotep arrives and causes a cave in trapping Alex in the cave.

Imhotep attacks Rick and Evy who race to find the treasure but are disappointed when it turns out to be gold and jewels. Alex is catapulted out of the cave, with the manacle assisting on the last part. Alex thinks he has found the scrolls and his earlier vision had come true. Evy pushes Imhotep off the cliff and discovers that the scrolls are written in middle Castilian.

Past Lives:

15 years (1921) earlier, Rick did some silver mining in South America.

Where in the World: Mojave Desert, England, and Cuzco.

Bestiary: The Caroupia.

Reliquary: Pizarro's treasure and the Castilian scrolls.

Notes:

The Chachapoyas are the tribe that Indiana Jones took the golden idol at the start of *Raiders of the Lost Ark.*

1-9 "Fear Itself"

Release Date: December 1, 2001

The Cast:

Alex O'Connell

Rick O'Connell

Evy O'Connell

Jonathan Carnahan

Colin Weasler

Imhotep

Writer: Steven Melching

Director: Eddie Houchins

Historical Backstory:

Genghis Khan stored his treasures at Mogoca, which may include the Scrolls of Thebes.

Plot Summary:

The O'Connells are at Mogoca to see if Genghis Khan had the scrolls of Thebes. They are disappointed to discover that Russian soldiers took most of the treasure to the Winter Palace near Leningrad. Imhotep arrives and summons a fire demon to attack the O'Connells. They quicky douse the fire and the manacle attacks Imhotep allowing the O'Connells to escape.

In Leningrad, they explore the Winter Palace. Alex opens a nesting doll which releases a gogul. The gogul is a creature according to Russian folklore makes your fears come to life and feeds on your terror.

The family begin to see visions of their fears brought to life. After defeating the gogul, they find a box with a page from the scrolls. They trap the gogul in a box and give it to Imhotep.

After escaping Imhotep, they examine the page which has the incantation "the power is within you."

Past Lives:

Jonathan reads Russian because he attended several of the top universities in Europe. Jonathan is scared of clowns.

Evy fell through a frozen lake as a little girl.

Where in the World: Mogoca, Mongolia and Leningrad.

Bestiary: The Gogul. Alex compares it gogul to a gremlin.

Jonathan mentions that a cold spot is a sign of a haunted house.

Reliquary: One of the pages of the Scrolls of Thebes.

Notes:

Gremlins were first mentioned by British aviators in Malta and India in the 1920s but popularized during World War II.

1-10 "The Boy Who Would be King"

Release Date: December 8, 2001

The Cast:

Alex O'Connell

Rick O'Connell

Evy O'Connell

Jonathan Carnahan

Guest Cast:

Jin Wu.........................Mona Marshall

Lin Chou.......................Robert Ito

Writer: Tom Pugsley and Greg Klein.

Director: Eddie Houchins

Don't I know you?:

Robert Ito: Appeared in *Quincy M.E.* (1976–1983) as Dr Sam Fujiyama and Professor Hitaka in *The Adventures of Buckaroo Banzai Across the Eight Dimension* (1984).

Historical Backstory:

Marco Polo reportedly had the scrolls and may have gifted them to Kublai Khan.

Plot Summary:

The O'Connells have discovered that Marco Polo may have taken the scrolls as a gift for Kublai Khan and travel to the Emperor's palace in the forbidden city. They meet a young boy Jin Wu and help him against men hunting him down.

Jin Wu is the Emperor of China and invites the family to the forbidden city as his guests. He opens the hall of mental cultivation to Evy and Rick.

Alex spends time with Jin Wu and joins him for Tai Chi lessons with Lin Chou the Emperor's teacher. Lin Chou offers Alex advice to assist with using the manacle.

Jin Wu talks to the O'Connells and discovers the location of the scrolls when they ask for help with the translation. Jin Wu takes Alex to where he believes the scrolls are. The awaken the Shin Shen which attacks them. Evy believes that they can use the Scepter of Hsien to stop the dragon and throws them into jail. Lin Chou frees the O'Connells and tells them that the Emperor and Alex must perform the ritual. Just then the dragon attacks and injures Lin Chou.

The family discover the dragon has lain eggs. Alex uses the manacle to retrieve the scepter and uses it to stop the dragon. The treasure turns out to be olive oil.

Where in the World: China.

Bestiary: Shin-Shen★ a dragon.

Reliquary: The Scepter of Hsien★

Notes:

This is the hardest episode to make work as is – in 1936 there was no Emperor of China and certainly no-one was living in the Forbidden City. The last Emperor of China Puyi (born in 1902) had been forced to abdicate in 1912 and leave the Forbidden City in 1924. From 1932 to 1945, Puyi was serving as a Japanese puppet in the province of Manchukuo.

The Japanese had taken over the Forbidden City in 1933, the treasures of the city were smuggled out of the city and by 1936 had been moved to a specially built repository. It would be the Forbidden City Repository that the O'Connells accessed.

Jin Wu is presumably a relative of Puyi that Lin Chou was training to try and restore the monarchy.

Kublai Khan is the grandson of Genghis Khan who we saw in the last episode had part of one of the scrolls.

1-11 "Howl"

Release Date: February 2, 2002

The Cast

Alex O'Connell

Rick O'Connell

Evy O'Connell

Jonathan Carnahan

Colin Weasler

Imhotep

Guest Cast

Sir Arthur Fenwick...............Nicholas Guest

Marie............................Jane Carr

Writer: Tom Pugsley and Greg Klein.

Director: Eddie Houchins

Historical Backstory:

In the middle ages, Irish monks translated the text of the Scrolls of Thebes.

Plot Summary:

After following a clue to Greenland, the O'Connells retrieve the chalice of Leif Erikson but wake a doki★, a protective spirit. After losing the doki, they take the chalice to the British Museum of Antiquities, where Sir Arthur Fenwick mentions some translated texts found in an Abbey in Ireland, these texts include a list of Egyptian texts translated at an Abbey near Polbushant★. Evy volunteers to travel to Ireland to collect the translation from the McTalford Abbey.

Colin Weasler confronts Sir Arthur Fenwick and learns where the O'Connells went.

In the village, the O'Connells are warned not to travel at night. They ride out that night and are attacked by wolves. Rick is bitten as the family escapes to the Abbey and begins looking for the texts.

Evy finds a book that mentions that Horus used the manacle to bring a ghost back to life. Jonathan finds a treasure room full of silver.

Rick begins reading at a high rate and is stronger and faster. He rapidly grows a beard and sprouts hair becoming a werewolf.

Imhotep attacks and we get a Mummy-Werewolf battle and Rick runs off. Marie from the village arrives at the Abbey and tells them that Rick will turn that night and werewolves hunt down those of their bloodline. They take the silver to the village where it is melted into weapons. Alex is coated in a salve to attract werewolves. Marie then gives Alex wolfsbane treated with werewolf saliva, which will reverse the curse. The only thing is the wolfsbane must be shoved down the throat of a werewolf.

A wolf attacks Alex and werewolf Rick fights off the wolf. Alex uses the manacle to restore his father as the village fights off the werewolves.

Alex jokes that they are off to Transylvania next.

Past Lives:

Alex recalls his grandmother telling him the woods were full of leprechauns.

Where in the World: Greenland, British Museum of Antiquities, Ireland.

Bestiary: Doki★ A protective ice spirit. Werewolves, leprechauns (mentioned only).

Reliquary: Leif Erikson's Chalice.

Notes:

Part of the werewolf lore is that it hunts down all its bloodline, and the wolfpack comes for Alex.

The line about Transylvania would suggest that vampires, and Count Dracula, may exist.

1-12 "The Puzzle"

Release Date: February 9, 2002

The Cast:

Alex O'Connell

Rick O'Connell

Evy O'Connell

Jonathan Carnahan

Ardeth Bay

Colin Weasler

Imhotep

Guest Cast

Simon Montgomery.............Thomas Dekker

Writer: Tom Pugsley and Greg Klein.

Director: Eddie Houchins

Don't I know you?:

Thomas Dekker took over the role of John Connor for *Terminator: the Sarah Connor Chronicles* (2008-2009).

Historical Backstory:

Horus, son of Osiris made the puzzle to guide people to the scrolls of Thebes. The puzzle was then broken up and the three parts hidden around the world.

Plot Summary:

Imhotep has located a piece of the puzzle of Horus, but Ardeth Bay steals the piece. Imhotep animates the rows of statues to attack Ardeth, he fights them off and escapes chased by a fireball.

Alex is in London hanging out with his neighbor Simon who reads comics. Simon sees Alex using the manacle to do his chores and Alex tells Simon of his adventures.

Evy has exhausted all her research but Ardeth Bay telegrams them to bring Alex and the manacle to help find the rest of the pieces. Simon has stowed away in the Zephyr, believing that because he has read Bram Stoker's *The Mummy* that he can handle himself and he mentions that the mummies in the movies are slow.

The O'Connells meet with Ardeth and when the puzzle piece is brought near the manacle, Alex has a vision where the next piece is hidden, the Arch of Sobekhotep.

At the Arch, Imhotep turns up and sets the Zephyr on fire with Jonathan and Simon inside. The bunker is buried under a fireworks factory. The fireworks open the hidden chamber and Alex grabs the puzzle piece. But the Zephyr is destroyed.

Alex puts the two puzzle pieces together and has a vision of the location of the final piece, the statues of Bahariya. They catch the train planning on sending Simon to Cairo. Simon asks Ardeth Bay if the Medjai are like The Secret Avengers, a comic he reads. Imhotep attacks the train, Rick and Ardeth fight him to cover the rest of the party's escape. Alex throws the box with the puzzle pieces out the window. Imhotep derails the car with the O'Connells and Simon as a train bears down on them on the other track.

Alex only threw out the box keeping the puzzle pieces and they ride camels to the statues. Imhotep creates a sandworm that eats Alex and Simon. Rick and Ardeth rescue the boys as Evy and Jonathan find the last piece.

Simon assembles the puzzle and hands it to Alex which creates a giant image of the Eiffel tower. The puzzle brings to life the griffin statues to allow them to escape Imhotep.

Simon has had enough adventuring and is happy to go home.

Where in the World: London, Egypt.

Bestiary: Animated statues, sandworms, and griffins.

Reliquary: The puzzle of Horus.

Notes:

Simon mentions Bram Stoker's *The Mummy*. Stoker never wrote a novel by that name, his mummy novel was titled *The Jewel of the Seven Stars* (1903 and revised in 1912) and was not filmed until 1971 by Hammer as *Blood from The Mummy's Tomb*.

By 1937, there were very few Mummy films – only *The Mummy* (1932) and *Mummy's Boys* (1936) were likely to have been by Simon. *Mummy's Boys* was a comedy starring Wheeler and Woolsey, with a fake Mummy. The trope of the slow Mummy came with the Kharis cycle of movies which first appeared in 1940. However, Simon may have been referring to the opening sequence of the 1932 Mummy, set in 1921 where the Mummy Im-ho-tep is awakened and moves quite slowly.

I was unable to find any reference to a British comic strip from the 1930s called The Secret Avengers. There was however an American series by that name from Marvel comics in 2010.

1-13 "The Maze"

Release Date: February 16, 2002

The Cast:

Alex O'Connell

Rick O'Connell

Evy O'Connell

Jonathan Carnahan

Ardeth Bay

Colin Weasler

Imhotep

Guest Cast

The Minotaur.......................Kevin Michael Richardson

Writer: Tom Pugsley and Greg Klein.

Director: Eddie Houchins

Don't I know you?:

Kevin Michael Richardson lent his voice to many animated series and video games including the voice of The Joker in *The Batman* (2004 – 2008) and Dr Hibbert in *The Simpsons* (2009 – present).

Historical Backstory:

Napoleon stole the scrolls of Thebes while in Egypt and took them to Paris.

Plot Summary:

With the Puzzle of Horus glowing when pointed at the scrolls, the O'Connells take readings from the Arc de Triomphe and the Eiffel Tower which points them to the Paris Opera House.

Imhotep arrives in Paris and mutates an organ grinder's monkey which attacks the O'Connells at the top of the Eiffel. In the fight Evy is blown off the top of the tower but is rescued by Rick. The family escapes and heads to the Opera House and discovers that it is built over the catacombs. No one goes into the catacombs because of La Bete d'morte (the beast of death).

They sneak into the catacombs and encounter a minotaur who kidnaps Evy.

The rest of the party follow and must split up. The puzzle shows the scrolls down one corridor and Evy dropped her necklace down the other. Ardeth Bay and Alex look for the scrolls while Rick and Jonathan go after Evy.

Evy learns that the Minotaur is the guardian of the scrolls. Alex and Ardeth use the puzzle as a key to unlock the scrolls.

Evy discovers that the minotaur was a Medjai.

Imhotep summons several Egyptian skeleton warriors to guide him through the catacombs who attack Rick and Jonathan.

Ardeth says the spell and removes the manacle before the minotaur attacks. Alex puts the manacle back on to save Ardeth. They convince the minotaur to help them.

The minotaur reveals that Napoleon stole the scrolls and the Minotaur stole them back. A Medjai mage used the power of Osiris to transform him into the powerful and immortal minotaur.

The minotaur, Ardeth and Alex fight Imhotep who begins the separation ritual, but Alex burns the scroll. Imhotep and the Minotaur battle collapsing the catacomb walls allowing the Seine river to flood them.

The O'Connells and Ardeth escape with only fragments of the scrolls. Ardeth suggests that they should consider the manacle an asset not a curse. The manacle could be a weapon when Imhotep returns, and Ardeth Bay offers to train him as a Medjai.

Where in the World: Paris, France.

Bestiary: Mutated monkey, the minotaur

Reliquary: The Scrolls of Thebes

Notes:

Did they miss the opportunity to mention the Phantom of the Opera, especially when Imhotep appears in a box seat scaring the cleaner.

Napoleon was in Egypt from 1798 to 1799, returning to France with many artefacts including the Rosetta stone.

This minotaur is different to the ones seen in *The Scorpion King: The Rise of the Akkadian* (2002) (game) and *The Scorpion King 2: The Rise of a Warrior* (2008) (movie).

Too bad the O'Connells never followed the lead to Paris in "The Black Forest," which they abandoned to find Albert Einstein.

Also too bad is that Evy never saw the scrolls as she has a photographic memory as we discover in "The Enemy of My Enemy."

The Mummy: Secrets of the Medjai

2-1 "A New Beginning Part 1"

Release Date: February 15, 2003

The Cast:

Alex O'Connell

Rick O'Connell

Evy O'Connell

Jonathan Carnahan

Ardeth Bay

Colin Weasler

Imhotep

Guest Cast

Sir Arthur Fenwick...............Nicholas Guest

Anck-Su-Namun.................Lenore Zann

Writer: Tom Pugsley and Greg Klein.

Director: Eddie Houchins

Don't I know you?:

Lenore Zann: The voice of Rogue in X-Men The Animated Series (1992-1997).

Historical Backstory:

Anck-Su-Namun was a high Priestess who nearly brought down the Pharoah after the death of Imhotep.

Plot Summary:

Alex is undertaking his Medjai training, he makes the wrong choice. He is rescued by Ardeth Bay, who lectures that a Medjai must follow their instincts.

In Paris, Imhotep escapes being buried in the catacombs and finds Colin Weasler selling a comic book about Weasler's heroic adventures with the Mummy. He is surprised to see Imhotep alive, and the Mummy transports them to Egypt.

In London, Evy is explaining why the Zephyr has been destroyed, Sir Arthur Fenwick is understanding as he had a few run ins with the undead himself. He sends them to Valley of the Kings, as there have been occurrences at some of the Museum dig sites and they can visit Alex during his training.

The O'Connells have a new Zephyr and fly to Egypt. They see Alex and Ardeth to take them to the dig sites and find that Imhotep is back, trying to break into a tomb. Imhotep steals the body in the tomb and resurrects several soldier mummies to attack the O'Connells. Alex uses the manacle to trap the mummies but is weakened.

They see the Corona of Izema which points to the Lake of Eternity – the water of which can resurrect the dead. It only appears for 24 hours every 5000 years. It explains why Imhotep was in a hurry.

Jonathan flies the Zephyr II and lands it.

Imhotep sees the O'Connells and uses his magic to throw rocks at the Zephyr II and the O'Connell party. It's a race to the lake with the O'Connells riding a log down the mountain. They ram the log into Imhotep which causes the stolen mummy to be flung into the lake.

They discover that the mummy was that of Anck-Su-Namun, a high priestess and the most dangerous woman in the world known as the Viper of the Nile. She nearly brought down the Pharoah after Imhotep was mummified.

As Jonathan is walking back to the rest of the party he collects some of the water of the lake,

Anck-Su-Namun has fire vision and can make giant crabs out of rocks. Evy and Anck-Su-Namun begin to fight with bamboo staffs as

Rick and Alex defeat the rock crab. The Mummies leave just before the lake disappears, The O'Connells are nearly sucked into void and ride a geyser out but the crash injures Evy, leaving her mortally wounded.

Where in the World: Egypt, Paris.

Bestiary: Soldier mummies, Rock Crabs.

Reliquary: The Lake of Eternity and the Corona of Izema.

Take That Bembridge Scholars!:

Anck-Su-Namun was a high priestess who was mummified after Imhotep and for her schemes was known as The Viper of the Nile. Anck-Su-Namun is no longer the Pharoah's mistress. This directly contradicts what we saw in *The Mummy* (1999).

Notes:

Weasler has had enough time to create several comics and sell them on the street in Paris.

2-2 "A New Beginning Part 2"

Release Date: February 22, 2003

The Cast:

Alex O'Connell

Rick O'Connell

Evy O'Connell

Jonathan Carnahan

Ardeth Bay

Colin Weasler

Imhotep

Guest Cast

Anck-Su-Namun................Lenore Zann

Writer: Tom Pugsley and Greg Klein.

Director: Richard Sebast

Historical Backstory:

Princess Nefertiri and High Priestess Anck-Su-Namun hid away the Scythe of Anubis. Another of Imhotep's crimes was trying to steal the Scythe.

Plot Summary

Evy has died from her injuries (as seen in Part 1), but the water Jonathan collected is able to resurrect her. Evy comes back different.

Imhotep tells Anck-Su-Namun that he is seeking the Scythe of Anubis.

Ardeth gives Alex some Medjai defense moves. They hear that the Mummies are attacking a ship in the Aegean Sea.

Evy begins to get visions of Princess Nefertiri and she reveals that Imhotep and Anck-Su-Namun planned to use the scythe and were both mummified for that crime. As the Zephyr heads to the ship Imhotep summons a storm.

Evy leaps on the ship tying the Zephyr allowing the rest of the part on board. Anck-Su-Namun brings some of the piping to life in the form of a spider to hunt Rick and Evy. As Imhotep hunts Alex, Jonathan and Ardeth.

Evy reveals that she is not Evy and that the water of the lake brought forth a past life. The boat is about to crash and the O'Connells climb onto the Zephyr.

Anck-Su-Namun leads Imhotep to the Temple of Anubis where Anck-Su-Namun and Nefertiri daughter of Ay it-Netjer hid it.

Imhotep finds the Scythe and empowers it as Anck-Su-Namun betrays him and steals the scythe. Evy/Nefertiri calls forth Anubis to claim his scythe and the god drags Anck-Su-Namun to the underworld.

After the defeat, Nefertiri retreats and Evy returns.

Past Lives:

Literally, as it is revealed again that Evy is the reincarnation of Nefertiri.

Where in the World: Egypt, the Aegean Sea.

Bestiary: Anubis, mechanical spider.

Reliquary: The Scythe of Anubis, the water of the Lake of Eternity.

Take That Bembridge Scholars!

Nefertiri is now the daughter of Ay it-Netjer instead of Seti I.

The historical Nefertari, daughter-in-law of Seti I, had the seal of the Pharaoh Ay it-Netjer in her tomb leading some historians to speculate that she was a descendant of that 18th Dynasty Pharaoh. Ay ruled from either 1323-1319BC or 1326-1323BC depending on the historian.

Notes:

Jonathan refers to Anck-Su-Namun as Miss Mummy 3000BC instead of 1290BC, but he may be exaggerating for comic effect or referring to the fact that she is about 3000 years old.

Rick and rest of the party are surprised about Evy's past life but Rick, Jonathan and Ardeth were informed about Evy's past life as Nefertiri in *The Mummy Returns*.

2-3 "The Dark Medjai"

Release Date: March 1, 2003

The Cast:

Alex O'Connell

Rick O'Connell

Evy O'Connell

Jonathan Carnahan

Ardeth Bay

Guest Cast:

Nizam Toth......................Michael T. Weiss

Yanit...........................Jeannie Elias

Fadil............................ Jeff Bennett

Habu

Salim

Tariq

Writer: Steve Melching.

Director: Eddie Houchins

Don't I know you?:

Michael T. Weiss played Jarod in *The Pretender* (1996 – 2001) and the voice of Tarzan in *Disney's The Legend of Tarzan* (2001 – 2002).

Jeff Bennet provided voices to many animated series including Professor Porter in *Disney's The Legend of Tarzan* (2001 – 2002) and Petrie in the *Land Before Time* series.

Jeannie Elias is a voice actor in numerous animated series and games including Pussy Galore in *Goldeneye: Rogue Agent* (2004).

Historical Backstory:

Nizam Toth was the only Medjai to betray the order. Ardeth Bay underestimated him and nearly lost his life.

Plot Summary:

Nizam Toth escapes captivity using trained rats and killing one of his captors. The O'Connells drop Alex back to Medjai training with Ardeth Bay. The other apprentice Medjai call Alex, the teacher's pet.

Toth returned to his magic hideout and recites a spell to return him to his prime. He then summons his jackal mummies.

Alex is undertaking his lessons about teamwork, but one of his classmates, Fadil, keeps sabotaging him and taunting him because Alex has no Medjai blood and is only there because he has the Manacle of Osiris.

Toth attacks the Medjai academy, just as Fadil and Alex are about to come to blows. The class all thought the Dark Medjai was just a legend. Alex tries to make a plan of attack but Fadil and his cronies rush in and are promptly defeated.

Toth sends his jackals to attack but Ardeth Bay arrives just in time. As Toth and Ardeth Bay cross swords, the Jackals become Jackal men and attack the students.

Ardeth is defeated and Toth puts a magic scarab on Ardeth's forehead, which puts him to sleep. Alex tries to use the manacle to rescue Ardeth but fails and sets the academy alight. Toth and his jackals escape with Ardeth.

The class saddles up their camels to rescue Ardeth but as they reach Toth's hideout, the group separates at a fork in the tunnels. Alex and Yanit take the left path and Fadil and the rest of the class down the right. The right-hand path is a trap as walls come down and the hall begins to fill with sand. Hearing the cries of their classmates, Alex and Yanit investigate. Alex tries to use the manacle to break the wall, but it is too big and heavy. Yanit estimates they have 15 minutes to rescue the others. Fadil believes that Alex is abandoning them as they leave.

The jackals attack Alex and Yanit but Alex outsmarts them by throwing a stick.

They find a bridge that says that "No man may reach the other side alive." Alex walks onto the bridge and sets off several pendulum blades. Yanit walks straight across revealing that she is a young woman. She then jams the gears so Alex can cross the bridge.

Yanit reveals that women are forbidden to be Medjai, but her father and grandfather were both Medjai and as an only child she felt she had to follow the family tradition.

The pair find Ardeth as Toth is asking for the Medallion and threatening with his trained snakes. Alex fights Toth as Yanit fights off the snakes. Toth and the snakes fall into a crevice and Alex and Yanit rescue Ardeth. Toth is clinging to the edge of the crevice and Ardeth reveals that if you remove the legs of the magic scarab it can read minds. Ardeth discovers how to rescue the others. They use Toth's flaming simitar to cut the bars on the trap and rescue the others.

Ardeth reveals that he knows Yanit's secret and is willing to allow her to join the Medjai.

Past Lives:

Jonathan attended boarding school.

Where in the World: Egypt.

Bestiary: Jackal mummies, electric snakes.

Reliquary: the medallion of the Medjai, the flaming simitar, the magic scarab.

Take That Bembridge Scholars!

The other students say that Alex has no Medjai blood, but it is revealed in *The Mummy Returns* that Rick was a Medjai. Also, in the next adventure "Like Father, Like Son" it is revealed that Rick's father is a Medjai also.

2-4 "Like Father, Like Son"

Release Date: March 8, 2003

The Cast:

Alex O'Connell

Rick O'Connell

Ardeth Bay

Guest Cast:

Jack O'Connell.................. Charles Napier

Scarab...........................Rene Auberjonois

Writer: Tom Pugsley and Greg Klein.

Director: Richard Sebast

Don't I know you?:

Charles Napier had roles in *Rambo: First Blood Part II* (1985), *Austin Powers: International Man of Mystery* (1997), and *Austin Powers: The Spy Who Shagged Me* (1999) as well as providing the voice of Zed in *Men In Black: The Animated Series* (1997 - 2001).

Rene Auberjonois: best known as Clayton Endicott III in *Benson* (1980-1986) and the shapeshifting alien Odo in *Star Trek: Deep Space Nine* (1993-1999).

Plot Summary:

Alex is on the Kobre nahaya★, a challenge to survive in the desert without food and water and find a Medjai dagger. As Alex finds the dagger a sandstorm appears, he signals for help but is crushed by the sand.

Alex is rescued by a man in a cloak and felt hat. The man identifies himself as Jack, legitimate treasure hunter. Jack asks about the manacle and Alex tells him the tale as they wait out the sandstorm.

The next morning, Jack tells Alex that he is looking for the Scarab Amulet and is close to finding it. They head to Jack's supplies, but a trio of hungry hyenas have gotten there first. Alex uses the Manacle to chase off the hyenas just as Ardeth arrives.

Ardeth, Jack and Alex head back to camp to see Rick, who reveals that Jack is his father. Alex says that Rick had told him that Jack was dead, and Rick says that Jack left the family when Rick was Alex's age - twenty years ago and he hadn't seen him since.

Rick is angry and pulls Alex from Medjai training and Jack leaves. Alex follows Jack to help find the scarab amulet. They find the temple canyon and the amulet. Alex tries to use the manacle, but the amulet is trapped in a pyramid shaped cage.

Jack uses a crossbow to send a rope across the chasm and the pair shimmy across. Jack uses an acid he got from an escape artist in Calcutta to melt the cage. Jack picks up the Amulet, but it bites him. That releases that Scarab creature inside the amulet. Scarab fears the Manacle which imprisoned him originally.

Jack and Alex shimmy back but Scarab cuts the rope. Rick arrives and pulls them up. Scarab leaps across the chasm and the O'Connells flee with Rick using dynamite to blow up Scarab and trapping them inside the temple.

They find wall paintings showing Osiris fighting Scarab with the manacle. Scarab tunnels in to kill them but the O'Connells use the tunnel to escape. Alex notices that Jack has a Medjai tattoo and Jack reveals that he was a Medjai in his youth.

Scarab spits an adhesive at Rick and Jack and attacks Alex. Rick and Jack, stuck together, must work together to rescue Alex. Scarab grabs them and crushes the adhesive and Jack throws the acid on the creature.

The O'Connells climb into the Zephyr and Scarab follows them and tears the Zephyr apart. Alex slices through the canvas causing the Scarab to fall to his doom.

Jack reveals that he ran away from his family and responsibilities, but he realizes that you can't run from your destiny. Rick allows Alex to continue his Medjai training. Jack mentions that he spoke to Ardeth, and he will be finding missing Medjai artifacts before they fall into the wrong hands.

Past Lives:

Jack left Rick and his mother twenty years earlier.

Where in the World: Egypt.

Bestiary: Scarab.

Reliquary: The Scarab Amulet.

Notes:

The Scarab Amulet is different to the Magic Scarab that appeared in "The Dark Medjai".

The Kobre nahaya, is different from the *Mushwar Wa* seen in *The Mummy Chronicles: Revenge of the Scorpion King*.

I love the fact the Jack introduces himself as a legitimate treasure hunter.

2-5 "A Fair to Remember"

Release Date: March 15, 2003

The Cast:

Alex O'Connell

Rick O'Connell

Evy O'Connell

Jonathan Carnahan

Colin Weasler

Imhotep

Guest Cast:

Sir Arthur Fenwick....................Nicholas Guest

Charlie Royce...........................Greg Ellis

The Rakshasa.........................John Dimaggio

Writer: William Forrest Cluverius.

Director: Eddie Houchins

Don't I know you?:

John Dimaggio: The voice of Jake the Dog in *Adventure Time* (2010-2018) and Bender in *Futurama* (1999 – 2013).

Plot Summary:

The O'Connells are in Sri Lanka searching for the Eye of Shiva, which can set clouds ablaze and send fire across the land. They find the statue, but the Eye is missing. There are claw marks and tiger fur on the statue.

Jonathan tries to steal a necklace but is attacked by a cobra. He tries to hit the snake but breaks the wall, flooding the chamber and releasing several very angry crocodiles. The O'Connells escape in the motorboat stored in the back of the Zephyr and radio Sir Arthur Fenwick. Fenwick tells them that Imhotep may not have beaten them a big game hunter just made a discovery at that temple and is revealing his findings at the Chicago International Fair. Evy suggests that Imhotep and Weasler are likely to be at the fair hunting for the Eye. Sir Colin says that the eye was forged in great heat and the only way to destroy the Eye is to freeze it.

Rick chastises Jonathan for being unreliable.

At the fair, Jonathan uses his skills to win a giant stuffed pink elephant by throwing a baseball into a basket and the family visit an Artic display, home to world's largest freezer. Showing off for Alex, Jonathan accidentally releases the polar bears from their display. Jonathan overhears Rick and Evy deciding to tell Jonathan to leave.

The O'Connells head to the Sri Lanka display to find that the hunter has found a tiger-man. Jonathan recognizes the hunter as Charlie Royce, who he went to college with. Jonathan offers to talk to Charlie as the others search for Imhotep.

Jonathan finds Charlie locked in the cage and frees him only to discover that the tiger-man is a shapeshifter, a rakshasa. The tiger-man breaks the desk looking for the Eye.

Evy runs into Charlie Royce who introduces himself as "the class of '28" and that Jonathan had set them up on a date.

Imhotep arrives at the fair but is angry that the O'Connells have beaten him. He tries to attack the Rakshasa, who is disguised as Jonathan. Imhotep is then dragged to perform at the haunted house by a fair worker.

The Rakshasa follows Charlie and Evy onto the cable cars, and attacks Charlie who hands over the Eye. Rick attacks the Rakshasa who drops the Eye out of the car. Jonathan catches the Eye just as Imhotep arrives. Jonathan and Alex flee into the hall of mirrors as the Mummy and Rakshasa fight over the Eye. The Rakshasa says the spell to activate the Eye causing a firestorm.

The Eye lands on the rollercoaster and Rick, Imhotep, and the Rakshasa fight over the eye. Jonathan uses a hot air balloon and gets the Eye, he then uses his carnival skills to throw the Eye into the freezer.

Alex gets a vision of Gibraltar.

The tiger-man escapes disguised as a firefighter.

Past Lives:

Jonathan spent a great deal of time at carnivals in his youth. Jonathan once took an Engineering course.

Where in the World: Sri Lanka - the temple of Shiva, Chicago. ·

Bestiary: The Rakshasa.

Reliquary: The Eye of Shiva.

Notes:

Jonathan complains that they are missing Uncle Reginald's clambake. Presumably, Reginald is the brother of Howard Carnahan.

Jonathan says that the tiger-man has eaten his spinach, a reference to Popeye.

If Charlie Royce graduated in 1928, he would have started his four-year degree in 1924. He would have been in several classes with Jonathan who may have been just starting at the same college as Evy. Evy most likely finished her degree (at Oxford as revealed in *The Mummy: Valley of the Gods*) in 1924 and began work in Cairo in 1925, where Jonathan soon followed, after dropping out.

2-6 "The Enemy of My Enemy"

Release Date: March 22, 2003

The Cast:

Alex O'Connell

Rick O'Connell

Evy O'Connell

Jonathan Carnahan

Colin Weasler

Imhotep

Guest Cast:

Aglaophone 1.................................April Winchell

Aglaophone 2.................................Kathy Najimy

Writer: Robert N. Skir and Marty Isenberg.

Director: Alan Smithee

Don't I know you?:

Kathy Najimy appeared in *Sister Act* (1992) and *Sister Act 2: Back in the Habit* (1993) as Sister Mary Patrick as well as one of the witches in *Hocus Pocus* (1993) and the voice of Sereena Secord in Disney Junior's The Rocketeer (2019–2020).

Alan Smithee is a fake name given when a director wishes to have their name taken off the episode or film.

Historical Backstory:

2000 years ago, the aglaophones tried to steal the cloak of Isis. The gods clipped their wings and imprisoned them in a mural.

Plot Summary:

Sir Arthur Fenwick has sent the O'Connells to Capri as he believes that Weasler has a lead on the Flute of Nephthys which will release the aglaophones, half bird half women creatures. The aglaophones were imprisoned in a mural after trying to steal the cloak of Isis, which can increase one's powers by ten times.

They find Colin Weasler at the mural with the Flute, Rick uses his whip and steals the flute but is too late and the aglaophones are released.

The aglaophones sing a song which allows them to control all the men. They chain Evy to the altar. They use the flute to reveal the path to the Cloak of Isis on the map mosaic on the floor and bring their ship out of the mural. Using their magic, they steal the mosaic.

Evy is trying to escape when Imhotep arrives. She offers to lead Imhotep to the Cloak so that she can rescue her family.

Jonathan is commanded to pull a lever to open one of the traps. Rick falls overboard and Alex uses the manacle to rescue him. The Manacle breaks the aglaophones' spell.

Evy and Imhotep are reluctantly working together.

The Cloak is guarded by a three headed dragon and the aglaophones use their slaves to distract the creature while they steal the cloak. Imhotep and Evy arrive, and Imhotep begins to battle the dragon. Imhotep and Evy follow the aglaophones as they play the flute to summon the cloak. The men battle the dragon as the spell wears off.

The men block their ears and resist being respelled. Evy plays the notes on the flute backwards which sends the aglaophones and the cloak back into the mural and Evy then blows up the mural foiling Imhotep. Alex gets a vision of a clock showing 6.30.

Where in the World: The Island of Capri.

Bestiary: Aglaophones.

Reliquary: The Flute of Nephthys, the cloak of Isis.

Take That Bembridge Scholars! Evy tells Imhotep that it isn't 3000BC anymore.

Notes:

Evy reveals that she has a photographic memory.

While the episode refers to the creatures as Aglaophones, they appear to be sirens, control men with their song, the men blocking their ears with wax to stop being placed under their control again (just as happened in *The Odyssey*).

In mythology, one of the sirens was reportedly named Aglaophonus (or Aglaope or Aglaopheme or Aglaonoe) which appears to be source of the name. It is unclear why the show didn't call them sirens.

2-7 "The Cold"

Release Date: March 29, 2003

The Cast:

Alex O'Connell

Rick O'Connell

Evy O'Connell

Jonathan Carnahan

Colin Weasler

Imhotep

Guest Cast:

The King of the Fodden.........................Keith Szarabajka

Writer: Tom Pugsley and Greg Klein.

Director: Eddie Houchins

Don't I know you?:

Keith Szarabajka appeared as the vampire hunter Holtz in *Angel* (1999–2004).

Historical Backstory:

The Vikings froze the entire village of Gunterfodden, home to snow trolls known as the Fodden.

Plot Summary:

In the Caribbean sea, the O'Connells are searching underwater for the Chalice of Augustus. They are attacked by a shark and ride some stingrays to escape. Rick uses the chalice to fight off the shark.

Fenwick then sends the family to a glacier in Greenland as a heatwave may have revealed the Trident of Voth. The Trident is a Viking relic that shoots a blast of unmeltable ice.

Weasler and Imhotep are in Greenland searching for the Trident. The O'Connells are searching on their snowmobiles and find the village of Gunterfodden, home to snow trolls known as the Fodden.

It becomes a race to find the Trident as Imhotep unleashes polar bears to attack the O'Connells. In the fight the Ice statue in town is knocked over and Imhotep thaws the frozen king of the Fodden, but Weasler has the locket of the Fodden. As Imhotep attacks Weasler, the Fodden freeze the Mummy. All the Ice trolls are awakened. They must obey the holder of the locket and following Weasler's orders, attack the O'Connells.

The O'Connells end up under the ice and ride walruses to escape and find the Fodden digging for the trident as Imhotep arrives. The locket is lost during the fight and Alex grabs it controlling the Fodden. As the fight continues, the trident falls down a chasm and the Fodden are frozen again.

Where in the World: Caribbean Sea, Greenland.

Bestiary: The Fodden.

Reliquary: The Chalice of Augustus, the Trident of Voth, the Locket of the Fodden.

2-8 "Time Before Time"

Release Date: April 12, 2003

The Cast:

Alex O'Connell

Rick O'Connell

Evy O'Connell

Jonathan Carnahan

Ardeth Bay

Colin Weasler

Imhotep

Guest Cast:

Captain Horoth.....................................Sherman Howard

Amar...Sean Marquette

Princess Nefertiri............................Cynthia Songe

Writer: Greg Weisman

Director: Richard Sebast

Don't I know you?:

Sean Marquette is the younger brother of Christopher Marquette, the voice of Alex O'Connell. He appeared as Robbie in *Black Mask 2: City of Masks* (2002) and as Johnny Atkins in *The Goldbergs* (2015-2021) and the spinoff *Schooled* (2019-2020).

Plot Summary:

The O'Connells have arrived at the Temple of Eternity and awakened the Sphinx, who challenges Evy to solve her riddle.

There is an earthquake and Alex discovers the Manacle has disappeared. Rick uses his whip to escape the Sphinx.

The family returns to the Temple and Alex discovers that everything has changed, and that Imhotep has been master of the world for 3000 years. Ardeth is a member of Imhotep's Royal Guard.

Imhotep is still human. He chastises the O'Connells for not solving the riddle of the Sphinx, tells the solution. He then blasts them with the manacle.

Alex tries to explain the situation to Jonathan and persuades him to help. The find a secret entrance to the Temple of Eternity and find the Whirl of Time, a time travel device. They activate it and jump into its energy. They find the temple is being constructed, the guards try to arrest them in the name of Imhotep.

Alex tries to trick the guards by Jonathan ruins it. Jonathan and Alex steal outfits from a clothesline and are discovered by a young boy Amar who offers them some clothes.

Princess Nefertiri has arrived in Nepata to secure the Manacle of Osiris after the theft of the Scrolls of Thebes. Alex confronts the princess to warn her against Imhotep, Alex and Jonathan are thrown in jail.

Imhotep tries to convince Princess Nefertiri to hand over the Manacle.

Amar helps Alex and Jonathan escape but the present-day mummified Imhotep attacks after he traveled back in time.

Alex makes it to see Princess Nefertiri and proves that Imhotep is evil. Nefertiri hands over a fake Manacle as a decoy for Imhotep to follow them back to Whirl of Time. Alex tells Nefertiri the solution to the riddle.

Imhotep is revealed to have caused the earthquake at the start of the episode and discovers that Amar destroyed the Whirl after they returned.

Evy is now able to solve the Riddle of the Sphinx which destroys the Sphinx. Ardeth reveals that the founder of the Medjai order was named Amar.

Past Lives:

back to the past to see Princess Nefertiri.

Where in the World: Nepata – The Temple of Eternity.

Bestiary: The Sphinx.

Reliquary: The Staff of Tremors, the Whirl of Time.

Take That Bembridge Scholars!

This episode takes up back to when Imhotep first fell out of favor with the Pharoah. This is completely different to what was seen in *The Mummy* (1999) and the basic details as revealed in the introduction to Season 1 of The Animated Series.

It may be that Imhotep was able to talk his way out of this and tried again later to steal the Manacle and the Scrolls.

In *The Mummy* (1999), it is revealed that the Medjai were formed by the Pharoah's guard after the death of Pharoah's death to prevent Imhotep being awakened. This reveals that Amar founded the Medjai.

The Riddle of the Sphinx is the same as the riddle seen in the myth of Oedipus. "What has four legs in the morning, two at noon and three in the evening?" With the answer being Man.

Notes:

Princess Nefertiri is drawn to look like Evy, but is voiced by Cynthia Songe, instead of Grey DeLisle, who voices Evy.

2-9 "Spring of Evil"

Release Date: April 25, 2003

The Cast:

Alex O'Connell

Rick O'Connell

Jonathan Carnahan

Ardeth Bay

Imhotep

Guest Cast:

Nizam Toth.........................Michael T. Weiss

Writer: Steven Melching

Director: Eddie Houchins

Historical Backstory:

Nizam Toth discovered a well of Dark energy and tried to get the Medjai to use the power. The Medjai elders refused his idea as it would corrupt the Medjai.

Plot Summary:

Alex is back at training and Ardeth reveals a new power that Alex can leap great distances. Alex is on the other side of the chasm as Imhotep attacks Ardeth and he must use his new power to rescue Ardeth. After a struggle Imhotep falls into the chasm and thinks that he can turn Alex's powers to his advantage.

Imhotep visits Nizam Thoth's hideout and attacks the guard. He awakens Nizam Toth to show him the location of the Dark Temple.

Alex is training with Ardeth and incorporating the new power into his fighting as Rick and Jonathan turn up. Just as the news arrives that Imhotep has freed Nizam Toth.

Alex is overconfident as they follow the trail. Imhotep mutates several rhinoceros to attack the party. Alex leaps out of the jeep and fights a rhino, but in his cockiness he fails to see a second rhino. His recklessness causes the jeep to be destroyed. As Rick and Ardeth talk to Alex he tells them that they are just jealous.

As they approach the temple, Imhotep mutates lions to attack the party and Alex rushes into the temple to face Imhotep. Nizam Toth and Imhotep team up and force Alex into the dark energy. Alex's eyes go black, and he becomes the disciple of Imhotep.

After the others defeat the lions, they find evil Alex who fights them. Imhotep orders Alex to kill his father who tries to reason with him. Alex overcomes the evil to Toth's surprise. Toth causes a flare of the energy which grabs Imhotep and drag him into well. Ardeth kicks Toth down the well. Rick blows up the temple covering the well.

Alex gets a vision of a djinn. As the temple disappears, Alex vows to keep fighting Imhotep.

Where in the World: Egypt.

Bestiary: Mutated rhinoceros, mutated lions.

Reliquary: The Dark Temple.

Notes:

Evy is at a conference in Cairo.

2-10 "Old Friends"

Release Date: May 10, 2003

The Cast:

Alex O'Connell

Rick O'Connell

Evy O'Connell

Jonathan Carnahan

Guest Cast:

Anck-Su-Namun.................Lenore Zann

Jane Sherman...................Gabrielle Carteris

Writer: Tony Schillaci

Director: Richard Sebast

Don't I know you?:

Gabrielle Carteris: Andrea Zuckermann in Beverley Hills 90210.

Plot Summary:

Jane Sherman is in the Temple of Sokhathai in Thailand. She sets off several booby traps and her local guides abandon her. She continues and finds the treasure room of Atwa Sagar★. A mummified Anck-Su-Namun appears and steals a ring and attacks Jane.

Alex is showing off to his friends with his Medjai skills on London Bridge, when Jasper nearly falls off the bridge trying to copy him. Alex must use his new abilities to rescue his friend. Rick and Evy talk to him, as he seems to still be a bit overconfident, pointing out there are responsibilities from wearing the Manacle.

Sir Arthur Fenwick arrives and tells the O'Connells that their old friend Jane Sherman has gone missing exploring a temple in Thailand.

The party is boating to the temple site and Alex is refusing to help navigate and Jonathan give Rick the wrong directions and they end up going through some rapids. Alex rescues them with the manacle.

They arrive at the temple and find Jane Sherman extremely aged and Evy says that Jane is the same age as her. They look through Jane's journal and find that she discovered the Ring of Sokhathai.

The party find Anck-Su-Namun, and she attacks bringing to life several of the statues. They battle and Anck-Su-Namun grabs Rick and sucks some of his youth restoring her. She then sets giant bat men on the party who grabs Jonathan and Evy. Anck-Su-Namun drains the siblings.

Rick and Alex go after their family and Rick chastises Alex for leaving them. Rick explains that they know he wants to grow up and make his own decisions, but they want him to be ready. They set off a booby trap of fireballs. Alex uses the manacle to escape the trap.

Alex and Anck-Su-Namun battle, and she draws off the power of the manacle from Alex. The adult O'Connells fight off the bat demons using the gongs in the temple.

As Alex and Anck-Su-Namun battle, the adults reflect the ring's power back on Anck-Su-Namun and Alex destroys the ring, returning everyone back to normal. Anck-Su-Namun disintegrates and returns to the underworld.

Alex apologies to his mother and she understands how he feels and is glad he rescued them.

The party then returns to London with Jane Sherman.

Past Lives:

Jonathan's nickname was 'Skipper' after he became the third-grade jump rope champion.

Where in the World: Thailand, London.

Bestiary: Statues, giant bat demons.

Reliquary: The Ring of Sokhathai.

Notes:

Thailand changed their name from Siam in 1939.

Alex seems to still be feeling the effects of his possession at the Temple of Darkness and hasn't lost any of the overconfidence he was displaying before that.

While not stated it is implied that Jane and Evy studied together.

2-11 "Trio"

Release Date: May 17, 2003

The Cast:

Alex O'Connell

Imhotep

Guest Cast:

Yanit……………………………Jeannie Elias

Fadil…………………………… Jeff Bennett

Writer: Tom Pugsley and Greg Klein.

Director: Eddie Houchins

Plot Summary:

Alex's classmate Fadil is visiting his family and playing soccer with his brother Salim as Imhotep arrives looking for the Nehansan*, based on information from Weasler.

Imhotep finds the Nehansan which is a giant spider created by the god Khepri as a force of destruction. Fadil's village guards the creature. Imhotep destroys the village.

Fadil works to save one of the village elders, who tells him that Imhotep will take the creature to the hot springs at Musurata.

Alex and Yanit are training at the Medjai Academy, Ardeth and the other trainees are out in the desert.

Fadil arrives asking for help telling them of the attack on his village. Yanit leads them to the plane that Ardeth bought as part of his modernization of the Medjai. She flies them to the hot springs where Imhotep has awakened the Nehansan. He sends a sandstorm with his face at the plane. They are able safely land and Imhotep sends the Nehansan to attack the Medjai.

The Nehansan releases hordes of baby spiders which Alex tricks Imhotep into throwing a fireball into. Imhotep and the Nehansan escape to Luxor, they follow in the plane.

Imhotep heads to the Aswan dam and uses a spell involving electricity and water to fuse himself with the Nehansan. The resulting creature, Spider Imhotep, attacks the plane and the Medjai jump in the dam and escape through the drainage tunnels. Alex uses the manacle to stop a turbine, but Spider Imhotep follows shooting acid at them.

The Medjai figure that with enough power and water they may be able to reverse the process and separate Imhotep from the Nehansan. They electrocute spider Imhotep and separate the two creatures and Alex is then able to destroy the Nehansan using the information about a weak spot that Fadil had mentioned earlier.

The battle caused a gas leak which exploded as they escaped.

Where in the World: Egypt.

Bestiary: The Nehansan, Khepri (mentioned only).

Reliquary: No relics this time around.

Take That Bembridge Scholars!

The Aswan Dam (now referred to the Aswan Low Dam) is depicted as a hydroelectric dam but the first plant (Aswan I) wasn't installed until 1960. However, there were hydroelectric dams at this point and the Egyptian government may have been trialing the technology – no doubt the explosion in this episode would have set them back.

Notes:

Yanit mentions that she has completed her training.

Alex is no longer getting tired after using the manacle.

2-12 "Just Another Piece of Jewelry"

Release Date: May 31, 2003

The Cast:

Alex O'Connell

Rick O'Connell

Evy O'Connell

Jonathan Carnahan

Ardeth Bay

Colin Weasler

Imhotep

Guest Cast:

Scarab......................................Rene Auberjonois

The Minotaur............................Kevin M. Richardson

Writer: Marty Isenberg

Director: Richard Sebast

Plot Summary:

The O'Connells arrive at an old Medjai outpost in Turkey which holds the Journal of Akeem, the journal of a former Medjai revealing many secrets of the Medjai. Alex gets a vision of Medjai medallions as Imhotep attacks.

Imhotep and Weasler escape with the journal and Alex races after them. Weasler activates the security system that threatens the others. Alex uses the manacle to stop the arrows as Ardeth arrives and helps the O'Connells escape.

Ardeth tells them that Imhotep is looking for the Medallion of the Medjai which is in Venice, Italy.

Imhotep and Weasler beat them there but discover that the Minotaur is now guarding the Medallion of the Medjai. Scarab is working with Imhotep and attacks the Minotaur.

The O'Connells and Ardeth arrive in Venice and discuss that one of Alex visions looks like Gibraltar. The Medjai keep their treasures in a secret chamber in the dungeons of a nearby prison. The entrance is underwater and the party dive off the gondola and swim through the tunnels.

Scarab attacks and he and Alex battle. Scarab uses the Nazim Nullifier, a jeweled Ankh, which takes away the power of the manacle. Rick rescues Alex and they trap Scarab in a cage.

They blast a hole in the wall and steal a speedboat as Scarab chases them. They blow up the boat, but it doesn't slow Scarab down. The minotaur and Scarab battle as they climb the Zephyr's ladder. The minotaur slices the ladder and Scarab falls into the water.

The minotaur reveals that he took over as the medallion's guardian when Nazim Toth escaped.

Alex is feeling sorry for himself as the manacle no longer works. The Minotaur sees a drawing of a djinn from Alex's vision and figure out that Imhotep is seeking to enter the underworld, Duat, and call forth the Djinn to conquer the world. The entrance is in Gibraltar and can be opened by reflecting the last rays of the sun.

Imhotep sends a waterspout and the Minotaur, Rick and Alex fall out of the Zephyr causing it to crash. The Minotaur attacks Imhotep, who loses the Medallion. Alex catches it just as the Scarab catches up with him.

The Medallion drops and Imhotep is able to use the Medallion to open the portal. Scarab tries to stop them following Imhotep (and if he kills Alex it's a bonus) but lands in an old munitions dump and Rick throws Alex a stick of dynamite which he drops onto Scarab. Just as the portal closes.

Where in the World: Turkey, Venice.

Bestiary: The Minotaur, Scarab.

Reliquary: The Medallion of the Medjai, the Journal of Akeem, the Nazim Nullifier.

Notes:

Imhotep found out about the Medallion of the Medjai from Nizam Toth in "Spring of Evil"

The Minotaur is the former guardian of the Scrolls of Thebes and was last seen in "The Maze" where he was caught in the collapse of the Paris catacombs and believed to be dead.

The Gibraltar vision occurred in "A Fair to Remember."

The djinn vision occurred in "Spring of Evil."

The time vision occurred in "The Enemy of My Enemy."

2-13 "The Reckoning"

Release Date: June 7, 2003

The Cast:

Alex O'Connell

Rick O'Connell

Evy O'Connell

Jonathan Carnahan

Ardeth Bay

Colin Weasler

Imhotep

Guest Cast:

The Minotaur..............................Kevin M. Richardson

Nizam Toth...............................Michael T. Weiss

Anck-Su-Namun........................Lenore Zann

Osiris

Writer: Tom Pugsley and Greg Klein.

Director: Eddie Houchins

Plot Summary:

The O'Connells blow up the rocks near the portal and uncover a path to Duat, which has 12 levels one for each hour of the night. As Alex points out that Imhotep has a big lead, the Minotaur reveals that he was entrusted with the secrets of Duat and there is a shortcut, but it is through the most dangerous parts.

Nizam Toth stalks the party looking for the Medallion. As Imhotep travels through the levels of the underworld, he finds the trapped soul of Anck-Su-Namun and leaves her there.

The Minotaur discuss Alex's abilities with Ardeth and how Alex may be more than just a Medjai. They arrive at the level guarded be the devourer of souls, an invisible snake, that Alex crushes with a stalactite.

Alex is told that Ardeth believes that he may be the Supreme Medjai. Osiris was the last Supreme Medjai. The Supreme Medjai has powers that come from within.

They must travel across the River of Truth, which leads them to the last level of Duat. The boat they use responds to self-doubt and will burst into flame. Nizam Toth attacks on the back of a giant scorpion.

Alex and Toth battle to stop Toth stealing the boat as the others battle the scorpion. Rick defeats the scorpion throwing it into the River of Truth.

Toth feeds into Alex's doubts as the rest of the party race and jump on the ship. Ardeth fights with Toth who falls overboard and is destroyed.

Imhotep arrives in the last level and awakens the djinn.

Alex explains his doubts to his father, which causes the boat to burst into flames. Everyone leaps onto the shore, and they find Imhotep and Weasler awaking the djinn warriors. As the rest of the party battle the djinn, Alex follows Imhotep to reclaim the Medallion of the Medjai.

The Djinn capture all the members of the party and Weasler gloats to Evy.

Alex accepts that he is the Supreme Medjai and can move objects without the manacle. Alex grabs Imhotep and throws him onto ground and buries him under a pile of rocks. A portal appears and sucks Imhotep into it. Osiris appears and tells Alex that he defeated the djinn and unlocked the power within. More powers will soon appear, and he must use them for good.

Osiris sends them back the land of the living. They state that Imhotep will no doubt return after forming new alliances in the underworld.

Where in the World: Gibraltar.

Bestiary: The Devourer of Spirits, giant scorpion, the Djinn.

Notes:

Alex is still wearing the manacle at the end of this episode, despite it being depowered in the last episode.

Presumably, the Manacle came off sometime during World War II as Alex is not wearing it in either of his next chronological appearances, *The Mummy: The Rise and Fall of Xango's Ax* or *The Mummy: Tomb of the Dragon Emperor*. Nor does he have any of the Supreme Medjai powers during those adventures. It is unclear how he lost the powers.

The Mummy: The Animated Series Game

The Mummy PS2 Game (2004)

Release Date: 2004

The Cast:

Alex O'Connell

Rick O'Connell

Evy O'Connell

Jonathan Carnahan

Ardeth Bay

Colin Weasler

Imhotep

Guest Cast

Scarab

The Rakshasa

Voices

Keith Wickham

Russell Bentley

Simon Greenall

Rachel Preece

Corey Johnson

Marc Silk

Writer: Julien Blondel and Kurt McClung

Don't I know you?:

Keith Wickham – provided several voices for *Thomas and Friends* including The Fat Controller.

Simon Greenall – provided several voices to *Tomb Raider II Starring Lara Croft* (1997)

Plot Summary

The O'Connells are on a dig. Jonathan complains that it is too hot, and they enter the crypt.

Alex uses his slingshot and Ardeth Bay gives him some training. He finds that Colin Weasley is in the tomb searching for the three fragments before the eclipse.

Alex tells his family, and they head to the Tomb of Kabahr★ and Alex goes ahead and finds Scarab guarding the first of the fragments.

Weasley says that he's heading to Peru, likely an Incan temple on the top of Mount Takan. They head there and Alex heads off alone and finds the second fragment guarded by the rakshasa in his tiger-man form.

Ardeth has a vision that the third fragment is at the Fortress of Mutsing★. Ardeth trains Alex in the use of the fire spells and Alex retrieves the third and final part of the talisman. As he puts the pieces together, Imhotep appears and tries to steal the talisman. They battle and Alex defeats the mummy, but Imhotep has Evy as a hostage.

Alex hands over the talisman but Imhotep casts a spell, but Ardeth takes the blast and dies. Alex travels to the Kingdom of the Dead to restore Ardeth.

The talisman pieces were blocking magical energy that Imhotep is planning on tapping into and the O'Connells explore the temples. Alex figures out how to block the energy and they return to temples Alex battles the Chinese Guardian the dragon.

The final battle is to be in New York under the Eclipse. Imhotep is on the torch of the Statue of Liberty and opens a portal to a spirit world, but Alex defeats him in time for the family to watch the eclipse.

Where in the World: Egypt, Peru, China, and New York.

Bestiary: Scarab, the rakshasa, a Dragon.

Reliquary: The Talisman.

Take That Bembridge Scholars!

Colin Weasler is referred to as Weasley. Clearly someone was a Harry Potter fan in the studio.

Alex doesn't appear to recognize the Scarab or the rakshasa.

Notes:

Why is the rakshasa, an Indian creature, guarding a relic in Peru?

This game was only released in Europe and had none of the voice cast from the Animated series.

The game manual lists the following powers for the Manacle of Osiris:

- Fire
- Ice
- Electric
- Shield
- Vision
- Telekinesis

There is no way to reconcile this adventure into the timeline of the animated series. This along with referring to Weasler as Weasley, would suggest that this is a fictional adventure.

The Mummy Chronicles

Revenge of the Scorpion King

The Mummy Chronicles 1 Revenge of the Scorpion King (2001)

Release Date: April 3, 2001

The Cast:

Alex O'Connell

Rachel Stroeker

Zorin Ungricht

Kommandant R

General H

Footrot, a pygmy mummy

Anubis

The Scorpion King

Writer: Dave Wolverton

Don't I know you?:

Dave Wolverton is a noted science fiction author and fantasy author, using the penname David Farland for the latter. He is also a lecturer and over 100 New York Times Best-selling authors have studied under him including Brandon Sanderson, James Dashner and Stephenie Meyer. His works include The Runelords, Serpent Catch, The Golden Queen and Ravenspell series. He has also written several Star Wars tie-in books.

Historical Backstory:

The events of *The Mummy Returns*.

Plot Summary:

Anubis resurrects the Scorpion King, four years after his defeat by Rick O'Connell. The Scorpion King is to be the intermediary between Anubis and the Nazis as the German High Command have tracked down the diamond from the pyramid at Ahm Shere.

Alex has begun his Medjai training with Ardeth Bay and is undertaking his *Mushwar Wa,* his lone walk and follows a group of Germans from

Aswan. Realizing that they are tomb robbers, he begins to sabotage their trucks. However, he discovers that he is not alone in fighting against the Germans, he finds Rachel Stroeker, a German Jewish girl. She and her father fled the Nazis, and her father is in the Foreign Legion.

They discover that the Germans are led by a treasure hunter Zorin Ungricht who has brokered a deal with Anubis for Hitler to have a thousand-year reign. They have returned the diamond that Jonathan took from the top of the Pyramid at Ahm Shere. Anubis agrees to their deal in exchange for the soul of one of Hitler's favorites, General H. In return, Hitler will receive the Ankh of Anubis which will keep him alive and victorious for a thousand years.

The party heads to Ahm Shere for the ceremony, the newly returned golden pyramid which is guarded by mummies and Anubis warriors. Alex and Rachel are captured by mummies. They are staked out in the hot sun for the scorpions to eat.

Alex has been able to palm a piece of broken mirror and uses it to free himself and Rachel. They manage to steal a car and escape. Alex uses a mirror to try and send a message to the Medjai.

After some discussion, the pair decide to stop the upcoming ceremony and use the parts of the car to make weapons. After blowing up the car, they return to the pyramid and disguise themselves as mummies.

Rachel is captured as the ceremony begins and General H relinquishes his soul into a jar. Footrot attacks Alex which causes a commotion. A flare is fired and, in the chaos, the jar with General H's soul is broken. The Scorpion King attacks Alex just as the Medjai army arrives and battles Anubis' army. Ardeth throws the Spear of Osiris and kills the Scorpion King again.

The Germans fly off and the pyramid sinks into the sand again taking the army of Anubis with it. Rachel stole the Ankh of Anubis in the battle and destroys it. Alex is given Ardeth Bay's Medjai dagger that was once owned by Saladin.

Ardeth returns Alex and Rachel to Cairo, where they arrive just as Rick and Evy return from England with the news that Evy has been offered a position by the Bembridge Scholars and moving the family to England.

Past Lives:

Zorin Ungricht once nearly killed Rick in a temple in India.

Alex first saw the Sphinx at age three with his parents.

Where in the World: Egypt.

Bestiary: Anubis, The Scorpion King, Footrot (a pygmy mummy), mummies, and Anubis warriors.

Reliquary: The diamond capstone of the golden pyramid. The Ankh of Anubis

Notes:

Alex uses several spells in this story all taught to him by Ardeth Bay. The story takes place in 1937 and Alex is twelve. These spells seem similar to the incantations that Alex uses to make the Manacle of Osiris work in *The Mummy: The Animated Series.*

The *Mushwar Wa,* is different from the Kobre nahaya seen in "Like Father, Like Son"

Heart of the Pharaoh

The Mummy Chronicles 2: Heart of the Pharaoh (2001)

Release Date: June 12, 2001

The Cast:

Alex O'Connell

Rick O'Connell

Evy O'Connell

Winston Churchill

Zorin Ungricht

Rachel Stroeker

Matt Harrill

Captain Bronson

Colonel Stroeker

Lord Harrill

Writer Dave Wolverton

Historical Backstory:

31B.C. After the death of Cleopatra, General Octavio entered Cleopatra's tomb to take her body and her wealth back to Rome. They are warned that there is a curse and that if any man of Rome touches the treasure they will die. Unable to take the treasure, Octavio burns the ship in the tomb. This ship was to take Cleopatra and her lover Mark Anthony to the afterlife.

Plot Summary:

On Allhallows Eve, 1937, Alex O'Connell is awakened by Winston Churchill banging on the front door of the O'Connell house in London to see his parents. He has brought a mummy that had been intercepted in Cairo. Treasure hunters had been trying to smuggle it to Italy so that Mussolini could fund his war.

Alex examines the mummy and finds a tag that identified her as Irani, the court magician for Cleopatra. Churchill tells Alex that the hidden

Tomb of Cleopatra had recently been revealed after a sandstorm and Mussolini had hired Zorin Ungricht to head the dig.

Churchill then shows Alex that Irani's heart is still beating. Irani comes to life and Churchill shoots the mummy and destroys one of Evy's vases. Alex returns Irani's heart, and she falls to the floor. Just then the O'Connells come home, and they are offered the mission to stop Ungricht which Evy willingly accepts, and Rick has to be persuaded.

The O'Connells fly to Egypt with a team of twenty British soldiers lead by Captain Bronson. Alex is unhappy that he won't be going to the tomb and staying at the Embassy. He is glad to see his friends Rachel Stroeker and Matt Harrill. Matt being the son of the British ambassador.

Alex sees Irani's shadow who shows him a Nazi spy watching the airfield. The soldiers are waiting on a truck to take them to Embassy so Alex asks if he can walk into town. Near the German embassy he finds Rachel and Matt spying on the Germans. The German spy spots Alex and chases the three friends but Irani's shadow helps them escape.

At the Embassy, Matt shows Alex and Rachel where they can eavesdrop on the adult's conversation and hears they plan to fly to the site landing on the belly of the plane to beat the Italians who have a three-hour head start.

The three friends discover that several truckloads of Italian soldiers are being sent to reinforce the initial Italian party. The trio try to warn the adults at the airport but miss the plane. They decide to get Izzy to fly them into the desert, but he isn't around, so they borrow his zeppelin.

They make good time but are shot down by Zorin Ungricht and the zeppelin crashes. Alex and his friends make it to the tomb with some guidance from Irani. They enter the tomb through a rear entrance but are soon captured by Ungricht, who tells them that the adult's plane crashed killing all aboard thanks to sabotage.

The Italians are looting the tomb, activating the curse placed on the treasure and waking all of the mummies in the tomb including Cleopatra and Mark Anthony. The Army of mummies attacks the Italian soldiers and drive them out. They allow the Italians to keep the treasure they looted to allow the curse to journey to Rome.

Just then the adults turn up guided to the site by Irani's shadow. Alex gives Cleopatra the old trawler that Izzy used in his zeppelin to allow her and all the spirits to journey to the afterlife.

Past Lives:

Rick shows the scars from when he met Ungricht at the Temple of the Monkey in Calcutta. Rick had a machete and Ungricht a machine gun. Ungricht won.

Where in the World: London, England, and Egypt.

Bestiary: An army of mummies including that of Irani, Cleopatra and Marc Anthony, Cleopatra's tomb has a frieze with Hercules battling a seven headed serpent. Statues of Isis, Hathor, and Anubis also appear.

Reliquary: Cleopatra's treasure.

Notes:

This adventure starts on Halloween 1937, with the majority taking place in November and we are told that the events of *Return of the Scorpion King* were three months ago. That adventure would take place in August 1937.

The Curse of the Nile

The Mummy Chronicles 3: The Curse of the Nile (2001)]

Release Date: August 14, 2001

Characters:

Alex O'Connell

Rick O'Connell

Evy O'Connell

Ardeth Bay

Matt Harrill

Rachel Stroeker

Zorin Ungricht

Hebekem

Nafi, High Priest of Osiris

Fatima

Historical Backstory:

5000 Years ago, a sorcerer, Hebekem, invaded the Temple of Osiris and tried to steal the tchet, an amulet formed from the backbone of Osiris. The sorcerer corrupted the amulet and became a djinn. The Priests hid the now corrupted amulet in the river goddess' temple.

Plot Summary

The O'Connells are sailing down the Nile with Ardeth Bay guided by Fatima, a young girl who found a golden censor from the lost Temple of Osiris. Fatima is attacked and Alex is thrown into the river. As he dived down under the water to escape the crocodiles, he discovers a sunken temple and a gold chain with an amulet.

Alex makes a wish to swim faster than the crocodiles and becomes half eel. He escapes and wishes to be human just as the ship returns to rescue him.

On board, Alex and Fatima identify the kidnappers who reveal that Zorin Ungricht hired them as he is also looking for the Temple of Osiris.

Alex hides the amulet from his parents and Ardeth before he collapses and becomes hospitalized. While unconscious, Alex dreams of the djinn who tells him that he has one more wish before he unleashes the djinn on the world. When he wakes, Alex is visited by Matt Harrill and Rachel Stroeker, and he tells them of the amulet and what happened. Not believing him, Matt grabs the amulet and wishes to be a giant slug. It works and the three reverse the wish just before the nurse comes in.

The three friends escape into the streets of Cairo and try to figure out what to do with amulet. The djinn has called Zorin Ungricht to itself, and the German has found Alex and his friends. In the scuffle Matt makes his third wish to turn Ungricht and his men into toads and frees the Djinn.

Matt uses the amulet to wish them to the Himalayas to escape the djinn, but the creature follows them. Alex uses the amulet to find someone who can help them stop the djinn.

The amulet takes them to the Temple of Osiris and the tomb of the high priest Nafi and awaken his mummy. The mummy says that only the pure of heart and unafraid can wield the amulet and returns to his tomb. Alex summons stone warriors to fight the djinn who has summoned dragons.

This fails and the djinn taunts him. Alex wishes to be as fearless as a Medjai and defeats the djinn. Alex undoes the damage caused by the djinn. He then calls on Osiris to reclaim the amulet as it is too powerful for humans.

Alex and his friends return to Cairo and discover that Zorin Ungricht and his men remained as toads. All the toads had been cooked and eaten except for Zorin who was being shipped to the London Zoo.

Past Lives:

Alex was born in Egypt.

Where in the World: Egypt.

Bestiary: Alex is turned into a half eel-man, Matt is turned into a giant slug and Zorin Ungricht and his men are turned into giant toads.

The sorcerer Hebekem becomes a djinn and uses fiery bats and dragons as weapons.

Osiris reclaims his medallion.

Reliquary: The tchet, an amulet known as the backbone of Osiris.

Flight of the Phoenix

The Mummy Chronicles 4: Flight of the Phoenix (2001)

Release Date: October 9, 2001

The Cast:

Alex O'Connell

Rachel Stroeker

Matt Harrill

Ardeth Bay

Ismael ben Jusaf

Baraba

Saramin

Writer: Dave Wolverton

Plot Summary:

Alex and two other initiates for the Medjai are taken to see an old woman, who is an elder Medjai. She talks to the candidates Ismael, Baraba and Alex and tells them that the Medjai had protected the tombs and treasures of Egypt for 5000 years and to prevent the supernatural curses and horrors from being unleashed on the world.

She then offers a test to become the flame which Ismael fails as he is not ready. The old woman has a challenge for Alex and Baraba, in the extreme heat of the summer an ancient threat has been awakened.

The old lady tells them that the egg of a snakebird called a phoenix in Egypt, draktferions in Greece and dragons by the Germanic people has been found. After forty consecutive days of heat, the egg will hatch. There are three days until that happens.

The egg is with a caravan of Arab traders, it is Alex and Baraba's job to retrieve the egg. As the pair leave on their mission, Alex discovers that his friends Rachel and Matt have followed him. Baraba is unhappy at this turn of events and separates from Alex and his friends to get the egg first.

The trio continue until they reach a river, Alex, and Matt head North and Rachel heads South. Alex and Matt discover the camp. Alex sneaks into the camp and almost has the egg as bandits attack and they steal the egg thinking it is a giant diamond.

After the raid Baraba rides into camp and Alex informs him that the egg has been stolen. Baraba rides off as Alex cares for an injured man. Ismael then rides into camp; he'd been following the other initiates to join their quest. Ismael, Matt, and Alex bury the dead and identify the men so that their families can be notified.

The trio follow the bandit's trail and find Rachel's handkerchief tied to a bush indicating that she had been captured.

The boys continue to follow the bandits to their hideout, where the bandits are celebrating their big score. They sneak into the fortress and find that Rachel and Baraba, along with many other prisoners, are being held to be sold into slavery. Alex determines that he has to free the prisoners and retrieve the egg.

After creating a diversion by setting some bullets off in a fire, Alex steals the keys and frees the prisoners. He then sneaks into the hideout and attempts to steal the egg. He is attacked by Baraba who wants the egg for the glory.

As Alex bests him in battle, Baraba alerts the bandits rather than let his rival get the egg. As the bandits capture Alex, Rachel and Ismael come to his rescue and threaten Saramin, the bandit leader. Alex throws the egg into the fire, to free the phoenix. The fire causes the egg to hatch in a blaze of light. The distraction is enough for Alex to escape and join his friends. The phoenix flies off into the night. The Medjai arrived having discovered that the trader caravan had been attacked and followed the flames.

A few days later, the twelve members of the Medjai council met in the old lady's cave to determine the fate of the three Initiates. After telling their tale, Baraba is told that he will never be a Medjai, but Alex and Ismael were not admitted but to continue their training.

Past Lives:

Alex is 12 in the first book set in August of 1937 and is still 12 during this book set in late July of 1938 – so Alex was born in either late July or early August of 1925.

Ismael's father was one of the Medjai who died in the battle against the Anubis warriors as seen in *The Mummy Returns.*

Where in the World: Egypt.

Bestiary: The Phoenix.

Reliquary: A golden statue of Horus, a bronze bow that Alex though may belong to Odysseus, gold chain, scarab amulet and a jeweled silver cup.

Take That Bembridge Scholars!:

We were told in *The Curse of the Nile* that Alex was born in Egypt but in this one we are told that Alex was "born in a far-off land."

The old woman tells Alex that he would be the first outsider to join the Medjai in many, many generations but according to the animated series "Like Father, Like Son" we discover that Alex's grandfather Jack O'Connell had joined the Medjai, and in *The Mummy Returns* it was hinted that Rick himself was a Medjai.

Alex is skeptical of the existence of dragons, but he encountered a Chinese dragon in the animated series episode "The Boy who would be King" and the Djinn in the previous book *The Curse of the Nile* had summoned a purple dragon.

Notes:

This four-book series chronologically sits nicely between seasons 1 and 2 of the Animated series as it shows the early days of Alex's Medjai training that was the focus of the second season. The only flaw is that Alex is never shown with the manacle or using it, although as pointed out several of the Medjai spells used in the first book are similar to the spells Alex uses to activate the manacle in the Animated Series.

The Mummy: Valley of the Gods

The Mummy: Valley of the Gods Issue 1 (2001)

Release Date: May 2001

The Cast:

Rick O'Connell

Evy O'Connell

Jonathan Carnahan

Ardeth Bay

Professor Julian Winters

Isop

Writer: Marv Wolfman

Artist: Mat Broome

Don't I know you?:

Marv Wolfman is a long-time comic writer with many writing credits including *Crisis on Infinite Earths*, *The New Teen Titans*, *the Tomb of Dracula*, and *Werewolf by Night*. He created Blade, Cyborg, Robin (Tim Drake), Raven and Starfire.

Historical Backstory:

During the Eleventh Dynasty (2150BC–1991BC), Isop, the high priest of Amon-Ra, has been informed that the Pharaoh has countermanded his orders and a mummification is taking place. Isop consults the Orb of Destiny to see the outcome of this act, the orb burns him and shows him that these mummies will rise again and destroy everything.

Plot Summary:

1927 Professor Julian Winters, an old professor of Evy's, is on a dig at the temple of Amon-Ra assisted by Ardeth Bay. He states that he has sent his research including the Orb of Destiny to Evy for her to look at.

The diggers open the temple and they attacked by a blue mist. The mist kills everyone except Ardeth and the Professor, who escape by blowing up the temple.

Next we see Rick and Evy are exploring a tomb and are attacked by a half man half scorpion, implicitly the Scorpion King from *The Mummy Returns*. The creature captures and kills Evy, only for Rick to awaken and reveal that this has been a recurrent nightmare for him.

The phone rings and Professor Winters is calling asking the couple to bring him the Orb of Destiny in Cairo. The O'Connells fly to Cairo where they meet up with Jonathan who joins them to meet Professor Winters who takes them to the temple.

Professor Winters explains that his men had been killed and that the Egyptian government is going to bulldoze the site, so they blow open the temple. The blue mist returns, and this time takes the form of animals. Rick grabs a stone tablet, and the mist creatures disappear.

Upon inspection of the tablet, it shows a map of Ancient Egypt showing the location of the Valley of the Gods. The party flies there and is confronted by two giant mummies.

Past Lives:

Professor Winters taught Evy at Oxford. Rick and Evy are on extended honeymoon and have been married for two months.

Where in the World: Egypt, Cairo, the temple of Amon-Ra and the Valley of the Gods.

Bestiary: The blue mist animals, the giant mummies.

Reliquary: The Orb of Destiny.

Take That Bembridge Scholars!: No changes to history.

Notes:

This was intended to be a three-issue miniseries published by Chaos! Comics as part of their Prime Universe. Ultimately, only one issue was published.

I reached out to the writer, Marv Wolfman, who graciously allowed me to read the scripts.

No Harm Ever Came From Reading a Book:

The script is much more detailed. Isop at the end of the prologue was killed by the Orb of Destiny. The script also makes it clear that Rick had been having his dreams of the Scorpion King ever since the Orb arrived.

No Harm Ever Came From Reading a Book:

Issue 2

Ad for unpublished The Mummy: Valley of the Gods Issue 2

Chapter 2: Beneath the Deadly Sands

Release Date: Unreleased

The Cast:

Rick O'Connell

Evy O'Connell

Jonathan Carnahan

Ardeth Bay

Professor Julian Winters

Writer: Marv Wolfman

Plot Summary:

Picking up after the cliffhanger of issue 1, more and more sand mummies appear and they take the form of Egyptian Gods including Ra, Horus, Osiris, Isis, Selket, and Anubis.

Evy is searching her bag as the sand god-mummies attack. Rick rescues Evy and lets off several shots at the mummies to no effect. Evy finds the Map that saved them in part one, but it has no effect on the sand mummies.

As the sand creatures grow in size they remove more and more sand revealing the entrance to the Valley of the Gods.

The party is about to die, as Jonathan holds up the Orb of Destiny which disintegrates the sand creatures. The party enters the tunnel, and they find glyphs of the entire Egyptian pantheon. Further along they find the preparation chamber seen in the prologue of issue 1, now filled with ten-foot-tall God Mummies.

At this point, trapdoors in the floor open and Evy, Winters and Ardeth Bay fall through. Rick and Jonathan save the rest of their party.

Winter packs up the chamber and flies it to New York. On the flight Rick falls asleep and dreams of Evy fighting Anck-Su-Namun and dying as the Scorpion King attacks and kills Rick.

Rick is rattled by this nightmare as Professor Winter explains that the Orb is giving him dreams of the future.

The party arrives at the New York Museum of Antiquities and Winters is unloading the mummies. Evy tells Rick she wants a night on the town. They go dancing and later a drunken Evy declares her love for Rick. Rick races out and calls the Museum and tells Professor Winter not read any spells not even a nursery rhyme. Winter promises that he won't say any spells, but we see him using the power of the Orb to wake the mummies and transfer his consciousness into the Ra Mummy.

The next morning, a very hungover Rick and Evy wake up as Evy races to the bathroom to throw up, declaring that this was not the hangover. Suddenly, the room explodes as fireballs hit. The couple flee but the fire follows them into the stairwell as a dust storm comes up the stairwell taking the form of Anubis. The dust Anubis can hit Rick, but he can't hit it. Rick is pushed out the window by the dust creature. The issue concludes with Rick falling to his doom!

Past Lives:

Evy mentions that the goddess Isis, the protector, was always her favorite as a child.

Where in the World: Egypt and New York.

Bestiary: the God–Mummies.

Reliquary: The Orb of Destiny.

Issue 3

Chapter 3 "If You Can Kill It Here..."

Release Date: Unreleased

The Cast:

Rick O'Connell

Evy O'Connell

Jonathan Carnahan

Ardeth Bay

Professor Julian Winters

Writer: Marv Wolfman

Plot Summary:

Rick manages to land on an awning as the dust creature dissolves. He looks up to see Evy being kidnapped.

Rick rallies Jonathan and Ardeth as they head to the Museum to investigate. Rick is convinced that Winter's mummies are responsible. Jonathan tries to reason with Rick that the mummies are dead, and Winters is on their side. But they find all the mummies gone along with the professor. Rick finds the Professor's home address and the three adventurers race to his apartment.

Winters is holding Evy captive and reciting Egyptian prayers and spells. Rick and party burst into the apartment as Winters possesses the Ra mummy. Rick and Ardeth free Evy and Rick grabs the Orb of Destiny. There is an explosion and Winters body disintegrates as the Ra Mummy's eyes begin to glow. Winters is now fused with the Ra Mummy. He resurrects the other Mummies until the appropriate souls can inhabit their bodies.

The O'Connell party flee as Ra-Winters blasts open the roof and the mummies fly off. The O'Connell party follow the mummies to the Museum as they travel on the subway Ardeth tells the legends that the Gods merged with men but grew tired of us and sought to destroy humanity. The Sect of Ahmad sacrificed their own lives to capture the Gods and bury them in the Valley of the Gods before removing all trace of the site.

Ra-Winters kidnaps Evy to merge her with Isis. Rick steals a motorcycle to chase his wife, Ra throws a fireball at a truck exploding near Rick. Evy screams as she believes her husband is dead.

Ardeth and Jonathan arrive at the scene and find that Rick survived as the truck blocked the explosion. They race to the museum finding the wall has been blown out and the guards knocked out to be merged with the gods.

Rick opens fire but the bullets have no effect on the god. Ra-Winters puts his foot on Rick's chest so that Evy-Isis can kill her former husband once the transference has taken place.

Rick realizes that the Orb of Destiny had reached into his mind, and he may be able to link with the Orb. He shoots a blast at Ra-Winters but finds himself in the Scorpion King's cavern. He fights the vision and begins to hit Ra-Winters with the Orb. The Orb breaks open releasing energy killing the god-mummies. The O'Connells run out the museum just as it explodes.

The police are on the scene and find that the mummies and professor have all been blown up. Evy is being checked by a doctor and reveals that she is pregnant.

Where in the World: New York.

Bestiary: the god-mummies.

Reliquary: The Orb of Destiny.

The Mummy: The Rise and Fall of Xango's Ax

Issue 1

The Rise and Fall of Xango's Ax Issue 1 (2008)

This four-issue miniseries was written as a prelude to *The Mummy: Tomb of the Dragon Emperor* released in the same year. All four issues were written by Joshua Jabcuga and art by Stephen Mooney.

Release Date: April 2008

The Cast:

Rick O'Connell

Alex O'Connell

Lord Horwood

Duncan E. Langford

C.J. Swetland

Orson Beaumont III

Plot Summary:

The issue opens with a newsreel of Duncan E. Langford, head curator of the Smithsonian announcing the disappearance and presumed death of Lord Horwood.

The story continues, on a train in Burma, near the Bay of Bengal. There is a poker game, and the players introduce themselves. Alex O'Connell is surprised that Lord Horwood, wearing an eyepatch, is alive, before hearing his father calling him.

Rick received a telegram that Alex abandoned the field trip to Africa he was meant to be on and tracked down his son, in the hopes of finding him before Evy returned home. Alex explains that he left the expedition to investigate Lord Horwood's death as he couldn't believe that the man he had read about in the pulps was dead. He was hoping to be Horwood's protégé or successor. Horwood, who knows Rick, is less than impressed that Alex had been following him.

At this point the train is attacked by undead ancient warriors riding rhinos. The warriors are seeking the Third Eye of Shangri-La, a giant blood ruby belonging to Xango the God of Thunder. The O'Connells and their companions fight the warriors and discover that Horwood was keeping the Eye in his eye socket.

The issue ends on a cliff-hanger that Xango riding on a Mammoth is leading his army onto the tracks in front of the train.

Past Lives:

Rick O'Connell met Lord Horwood at some point and did not form a favorable opinion.

Where in the World: Burma, near the Bay of Bengal.

Bestiary: Undead white rhinos, undead soldiers, and a woolly mammoth.

Reliquary: The Third Eye of Shangri-La.

Notes:

The Mummy: Tomb of the Dragon Emperor has the Eye of Shangri-La, and this has the Third Eye of Shangri-La, it seems likely that there is a Second Eye of Shangri-La.

Mathayus has blood rubies in *The Scorpion King*.

Xango ruled sometime between the 12th and 15th Century and the Mammoth went extinct about 4000 years ago presumably the mammoth was revived by Xango's magics.

Issue 2

The Rise and Fall of Xango's Ax Issue 2 (2008)

Release Date: May 2008

The Cast:

Rick O'Connell

Alex O'Connell

Evy O'Connell

Lord Horwood

J.C. Swetland

Historical Backstory:

Xango tells of receiving the Third Eye of Shangri-La as a wedding gift from his father. When Xango ascends the throne, he inherits his father's ruby encrusted ax. He became cruel and tyrannical trying to take over the world. He is poisoned by his wife, who ruled peacefully and was buried with Xango's Ax.

Plot Summary:

After the train crash, the O'Connell's and some of their companions escape into the ruby mines and take the Eye away from Lord Horwood. After being attacked by the mammoth, the O'Connells lose the Eye and Xango adds it to his crown and is restored in body and powers. He summons a giant plant to capture the O'Connells and Swetland.

Past Lives:

Lord Horwood is aware of Evy.

Where in the World: Burma.

Bestiary: Undead mammoths.

Reliquary: The third Eye of Shangri-La, Xango's ruby encrusted ax (mentioned only).

Notes:

Evy appears only writing a letter to Rick and Alex saying that she'll be home sooner than she thought to see both her boys – this is odd as Rick states in issue 1 that while Evy was on a dig and Alex was on a school excursion in Africa that he would be home alone.

Issue 3

The Rise and Fall of Xango's Ax Issue 3 (2008)

Release Date: June 2008

The Cast:

> Rick O'Connell
>
> Alex O'Connell
>
> Lord Horwood
>
> Duncan E. Langford
>
> C.J. Swetland
>
> Xango

Plot Summary:

The O'Connells and Swetland are rescued by Duncan Langford, head curator of the Smithsonian, who is leading a rescue party to find Lord Horwood.

The party follows Xango in a truck and eventually use hang gliders after the truck breaks down. The gilders are attacked by giant bats.

Xango returns to his now ruined city, uncovers his wife's tomb, and reclaims his ax.

Where in the World: Burma.

Bestiary: Giant bats.

Reliquary: Xango's Ax.

Issue 4

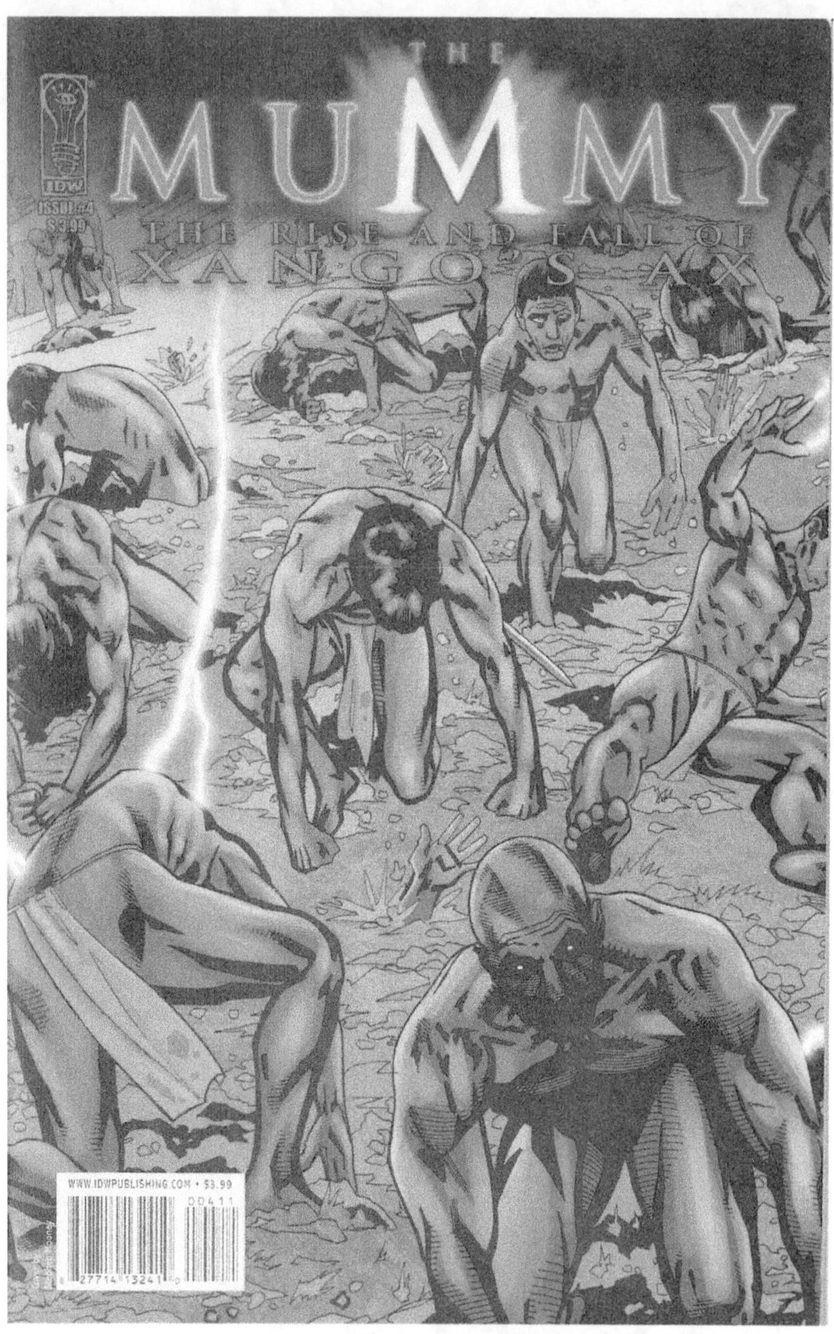

The Rise and Fall of Xango's Ax Issue 4 (2008)

Release Date: July 2008

The Cast:

Rick O'Connell

Alex O'Connell

Lord Horwood

Duncan E. Langford

C.J. Swetland

Xango

Plot Summary:

Xango has retrieved his ax and is going to sacrifice his prisoners. Lord Horwood attempts to bargain with Xango stating that he needs greater firepower. Xango resurrects more soldiers.

Alex finds a German tank and together with his father, Langford and Swetland, they attack Xango and his men. Swetland steals Xango's crown before Xango is decapitated by his resurrected father and wife. The resurrected bodies return to dust after Xango's death.

The O'Connells, Langford and Swetland trek eight days into Asia before finding a plane and returning to civilization. Langford hires Swetland to work for the Smithsonian. The O'Connells head back to England.

The story ends with a newsreel of Langford again reporting Horwood presumed dead, and the Smithsonian is restoring and preserving the relics of Xango's kingdom. We see Lord Horwood in the audience laughing.

Where in the World: Burma.

Bestiary: The mammoth brad undead warriors.

Notes:

The historical Xango hailed from the Oyo kingdom, in what is now Benin and Nigeria, on the west coast of Africa, which is over 6200 miles (10 000 kilometers) directly East of Burma in a straight line.

It is suggested that Xango's Queen may have been buried far from the Oyo Kingdom to prevent Xango's Ax to be used by those who wish to use it as symbol of power.

In this issue, after retrieving his ax, Xango says that his army will follow the path of sun and only stop when the land becomes familiar again. Given that Burma is East of the Oyo Kingdom this is going to be a very long trip unless Xango meant to head back along the path of the sun, heading West.

The Scorpion King Franchise

In "The Rock Reacts to *The Scorpion King*" Dwayne Johnston revealed that during the filming of *The Mummy Returns* (2001), the studio was watching the dailies from filming and decided to spin-off The Scorpion King in his own movie with the intent of making a franchise.

The next movie the prequel *The Scorpion King 2: The Rise of a Warrior* was a direct to DVD movie released in 2008 at the same time as the theatrical release of *The Mummy: Tomb of the Dragon Emperor*.

Four years later, Victor Webster took over the role of Mathayus for *The Scorpion King 3: Battle for Redemption* and reprised the role for *The Scorpion King 4: Quest for Power* in 2015.

Most surprisingly, 2018 saw the last of the Scorpion King franchise, *Scorpion King Book Of Souls*. This came after the 2017 reboot of the Mummy franchise for the Dark Universe.

In 2020, Dwayne Johnson advised that he would be producing a reboot of the Scorpion King set in the modern day. Johnson would not reprise the role.

The Scorpion King

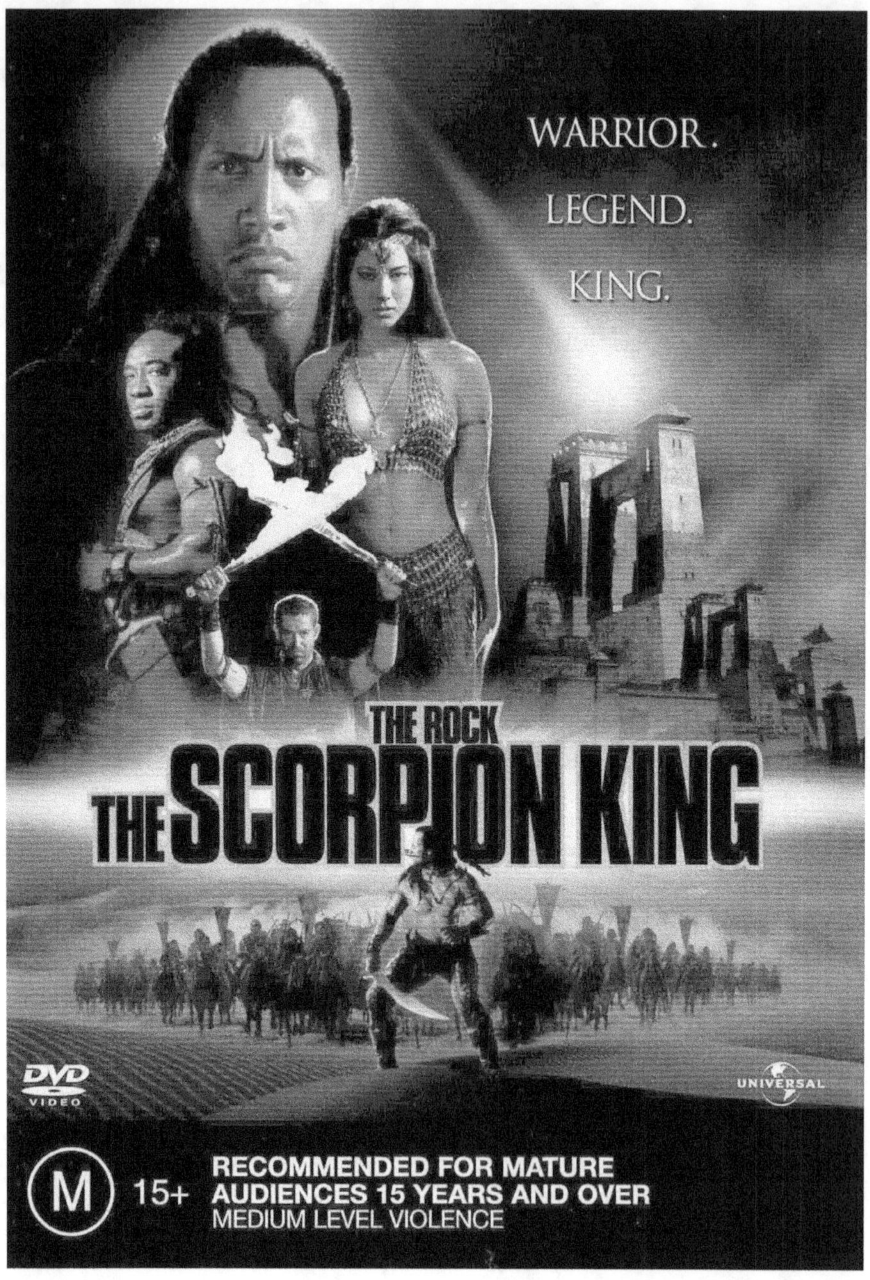

The Scorpion King (2002)

Release Date: April 18, 2002

The Cast:

Mathayus ....Dwayne "the Rock" Johnson

Cassandra The Sorceress.........Kelly Hu

Memnon....................................Steven Brand

Balthazar.................................Michael Clarke Duncan

Arpid..Grant Hesloc

Philos.......................................Bernard Hill

Takmet.....................................Peter Facinelli

Thorak...................................... Ralf Moeller

Jesup.......................................Branscombe Richmond

King Pheron..............................Roger Rees

Queen Isis...............................Sherri Howard

Writer Stephen Sommers. William Osborne and David Hayter

Director Chuck Russell

Don't I know you?:

Chuck Russell also directed *Nightmare on Elm Street 3: The Dream Warriors* (1987), *The Mask* (1994) and *The Eraser* (1996).

Kelly Hu has appeared in many movies and TV series including Inspector Michelle Chan in *Nash Bridges* (1997–1998) and Chen Pei in *Martial Law* (1998-2000), Lady Deathstrike in *X2: X-Men United* (2003), Cheshire in *Young Justice* (2011-2019) and China White in *Arrow* (2012-2020) as well as the role of Leilani in *Finding 'Ohana* (2021).

Peter Facinelli played the Cullen family patriarch, Dr Carlyle Cullen in the five movie *Twilight Saga* (2008 – 2012) and Maxwell Lord in *Supergirl* (2015-2016).

Michael Clarke Duncan appeared as Bear in *Armageddon* (1998), John Coffey in *The Green Mile* (1999), The Kingpin in *Daredevil* (2003), and Leo Knox in *The Finder* (2013).

Branscombe Richmond played Bobby in *Renegade* (1992-1997) and Kimo in *Finding 'Ohana* (2021).

Historical Backstory:

Before the time of the pyramids, Memnon leader of the hoard has swept across the land, thanks to the predictions of his sorcerer.

The Akkadians are reported to have died out long ago.

Plot Summary:

Jesup, one of the last Akkadians, has been captured and his brother Mathayus comes to rescue him.

Meanwhile the leaders of the remaining free tribes are meeting to determine how to fight Memnon, King Pheron has hired the last three Akkadians to kill the sorcerer for the price of 20 blood rubies. This questioned by his son Prince Takmet. The Akkadians accept the contract

The Akkadians head to Memnon's camp to kill the Sorcerer. Sneaking into the camp, Mathayus discovers Arpid, a horse thief, being tortured by soldiers.

It turns out that the camp is a trap, one of the Akkadians (Rama) is killed and Jesup seriously wounded. Mathayus escapes and discovers that the sorcerer is in fact a sorceress and discover that Prince Takmet has betrayed them.

Memnon kills Jesup in front of Mathayus. He is about to kill Mathayus, but the sorceress declares that Mathayus will not die by Memnon's hand nor any hand he commands. Memnon's solution is to bury Mathayus and Arpid up to their necks for fire ants to kill them. The pair escape and head after Memnon to avenge the death of Jesup.

To gain entry to Gomorrah, Mathayus claims to be bringing Arpid in for the bounty on his head. Mathayus is exploring the city, when his pouch of blood rubies is stolen by a gang of child thieves. He chases down the main thief and spares his life in return for passage into Memnon's castle. There they meet the alchemist, Philos, who guides them to Memnon in the training courtyard.

Memnon displays his prowess capturing an arrow shot at him with his bare hands. Mathayus is torn between killing an unsuspecting Memnon or saving the life of his young guide, who has been captured. Mathayus saves his guide and runs back to the alchemist and uses his catapult to escape flying into Memnon's harem. The women disarm Mathayus and during a battle with the guards Mathayus leaps from the tower and lands in the Sorceress' bath. He kidnaps her through the drainage system.

His plan is use her as bait to draw out Memnon and sets a trap in the Valley of the Dead. Memnon sends Thorak and his elite guards with an arrow dipped in scorpion venom.

In the Valley of the Dead, Mathayus is disappointed that Memnon didn't come and uses the cover of a sandstorm to attack the Red Guard and a cave to kill the guardsmen one by one until only Thorak is left. With his dying breath, Thorak stabs Mathayus with the poisoned arrow.

The Sorceress uses her magic to heal Mathayus declaring that he will have the blood of the scorpion in his veins. A recovered Mathayus sends a falcon with a message for Memnon that he is coming for him.

Mathayus and his party discover the alchemist who has perfected his Chinese formula, gunpowder. They head to an oasis and find the kingdom of Balthazar, the Nubian king, which is a haven for all of Memnon's enemies. Balthazar fights with Mathayus and as Balthazar refuses to yield, Mathayus makes a speech that they should work together to fight Memnon.

The Sorceress has a vision (where we discover that her name is Cassandra) that Memnon will kill everyone at the oasis. Telling Mathayus, she gets another vision that he will die in battle with Memnon. Cassandra steals Mathayus' camel and returns to Memnon.

At the feast before the big battle, Cassandra appears to placate Memnon's soldiers. Mathayus and his forces ride into the city disguised as dancing girls.

Memnon tests Cassandra's powers. She attacks him just as Mathayus arrives. The battle begins throughout the palace. Balthazar kills the prince. Mathayus and Memnon battle and Cassandra sees her vision come to pass as Mathayus is shot with an arrow. The Warrior pulls out the arrow and uses it to shoot Memnon. At that point, the gunpowder explodes and kills Memnon.

Under the rules of the hoard, Mathayus is their new king. Balthazar refers to him as Scorpion King as he leaves the next day. Cassandra is his queen and declares that there will be a long period of prosperity.

Past Lives:

Jesup and Mathayus share the same mother.

Where in the World: Gomorrah.

Bestiary: The Sorceress with her powers of prophecy and healing.

Reliquary: None surprisingly.

No Harm Ever Came From Reading a Book:

The novelization by Max Allan Collins tells us that Mathayus' cloak in the opening scene is Yeti fur. Yetis would later appear in *The Mummy: Tomb of the Dragon Emperor* (2008).

Take That Bembridge Scholars!:

There several historical and mythological men named Memnon. One is the King of Ethiopia who battled Achilles during the Trojan War. This battle is dated c. 1260–1180 BC nearly two thousand years after the events in *The Scorpion King*

Notes:

The Scorpion King: Rise of the Akkadian reveals that the third Akkadian is named Rama and that he is the middle brother between Jesup and Mathayus.

The Scorpion King 2: The Rise of A Warrior

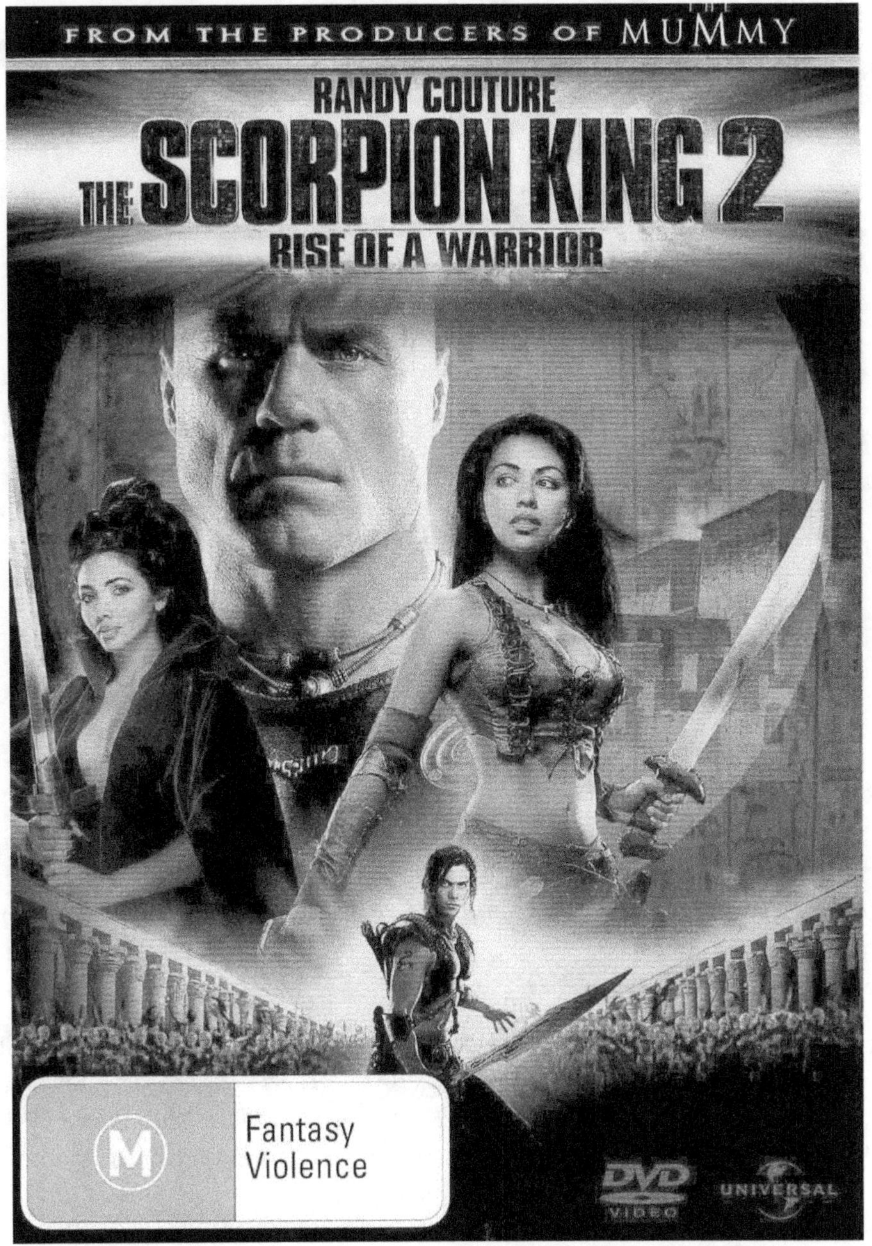

The Scorpion King 2: The Rise of a Warrior (2008)

Release Date: September 3, 2008

The Cast:

Young Mathayus......................Pierre Marias

Young Layla..........................Abbie Maybanks

Mathayus.............................Michael Copon

Layla.................................Karen David

Ari...................................Simon Quarterman

Sargon................................Randy Couture

Fong..................................Tom Wu

Ashur.................................Peter Butler

Inanna................................Terry Norton

Astarte...............................Natalie Becker

Writer Randall McCormick

Director Russell Mulcahy

Don't I know you?:

Russell Mulcahy – This Australian director got his start directing music videos before directing *Razorback* (1984) in Australia, he moved to Hollywood where he directed *Highlander* (1986), *Tale of the Mummy* (aka *Talos the Mummy*) (1998), *The Curse of King Tut's Tomb* (2006) and producing and directing *Teen Wolf* (2011-2017).

Pierre Marias – This South African actor worked as a stunt double in *Home Alone 4: Taking Back the House* (2002), *The Three Investigators* series (2006 and 2009) as well as acting in *King Solomon's Mines* (2004) and *Wake of Death* (2004). Since then, he has performed on Broadway starring in *Aladdin* as well as touring with *Rock of Ages*, *A Chorus Line* and *Flashdance the Musical*.

Michael Copon – The Blue Power Ranger in *Time Force Power Ranger* (2001-2002) also had roles in *One Tree Hill* (2004-2005) and *The Bay* (2018 - 2020) and its spinoff *yA* (2020).

Randy Couture – This UFC star also appeared in *The Expendables* series.

Historical Backstory:

In ancient times, Akkad was a powerful kingdom with Nippon as its capital. Their elite warriors The Black Scorpions, were prized as bodyguards for kings. The most honored was Ashur, but he refused to allow his son Mathayus to try out for the Black Scorpions and train for six years.

Mathayus disguises himself to try out and finds that one of the local girls, Layla, has also disguised herself and tried out. When the Black Scorpion's training master, Sargon tries to throw Layla out, Mathayus attacks Sargon. Ashur comes to his son's aid and he and Sargon start to fight.

King Hammurabi stops the fight and orders that Mathayus join the Back Scorpions. Sargon enraged uses black magic and sends scorpions to attack and kill Ashur. Mathayus swears vengeance and trains to become the greatest Black Scorpion.

Plot Summary

Mathayus returns to Nippon after the six years of training as a Black Scorpion. Mathayus is greeted by his mother and brother Noah and is told that Enki left home last year to make his fortune. Layla greets her old friend. King Sargon arrives to inspect the troops and Noah mentions that Hammurabi's death was suspicious. Sargon orders Mathayus to the palace for a special mission. Sargon wants Mathayus as his personal bodyguard. Mathayus' first job to prove his loyalty to Sargon is to kill Noah for speaking out against the king. Mathayus frees his brother, and the pair battle the king's guard. Mathayus throws spear at Sargon, but he uses magic to stop it and the brothers flee the scene, Sargon enchants an arrow, and it homes in on the brothers, killing Noah.

Mathayus heads to the nearest port followed by Leela who is fleeing an arranged marriage. She reveals that Sargon worships the Dark Gods which gives him powers. Mathayus and Layla board a ship headed to

Egypt. Layla states she is going to Egypt to see the pyramids. Mathayus is going to see the Pharoah to borrow the Spear of Osiris to kill Sargon, as Ashur once saved the Pharoah's life.

Aristophanes of Naxos, known as Ari, overhearing this tells Mathayus that the Spear won't work as it only kills Egyptian monsters, he suggests weapons the hammer of Zeus, the shield of Cronus, before deciding on the sword of Damocles. the sword was transformed by a bolt of lightning from Zeus and gifted to the queen of the underworld, Astarte.

Ari guides them into the palace them to the labyrinth which has a portal to the underworld.

They are joined by a group of prisoners in the labyrinth, including Pollux and Fong. The party must fight and kill the minotaur before descending into the underworld. Gilgamesh and Herodotus previously made the trip according to Ari, who guides them through the underworld. Ari tells them that they have one hour before they turn to stone.

The party encounters several challenges losing many of their party before encountering the goddess Astarte. Astarte and Layla fight while the rest of the party searches for the sword. To save Layla, Mathayus swears to build Astarte a temple, but she offers to keep him as her concubine. Mathayus says that he has already made a vow to Shamash to avenge his father. They escape with the sword with Pollux, just running out of time, turns to stone. Mathayus, Layla, Ari, and Fong are the only ones to return to the surface.

Astarte appears to Sargon and tells him that Mathayus will return and try to kill him. She grants Sargon extra powers in return for sacrificing all his people. Mathayus and Ari arrive in Nippon to face Sargon while Layla and Fong try to prevent the sacrifice.

Sargon appears as Ashur to trick Mathayus. It is revealed that Sargon hired Ari to lead Mathayus to the underworld so that Sargon could obtain the sword to increase his power.

Ari betrays Sargon giving Mathayus the sword and Sargon transforms into a giant, invisible scorpion. They battle, and Mathayus loses the sword. Mathayus is stung by the scorpion. He coats the beast in oil so he can see it and kills Sargon with the sword.

Meanwhile, Layla and Fong are at the amphitheater where all of Sargon's subjects have been herded. The pair discover that the crowd is to be sprayed with oil and set on fire with flaming arrows. Together they stop the oil from igniting and save everyone.

Astarte appears before Mathayus, reclaims her sword, and spares him knowing he will die soon enough from the scorpion venom.

Surprisingly, Mathayus awakens after being in a coma for three days. His mother, Inanna had been praying for her son to Shamash.

Mathayus then finds that Shalmaneser, the son of Hammurabi, has been made the new king of Akkad and that Ari had left for Olympia chasing Neptune's trident.

We see Mathayus riding off into the sunset on a camel.

Past Lives:

Mathayus is 19 at the time the main adventure, making him 13 in the prologue.

Where in the World: Akkad, Knossos, and the underworld.

Bestiary: Griffon statues, Winged scarabs, Sphinxes, and cursed mummies (mentioned), The minotaur, Astarte, creatures of the underworld.

Reliquary: Spear of Osiris, the hammer of Zeus, the shield of Cronos, a cloak and the Sword of Damocles, Neptune's trident.

Take That Bembridge Scholars!

In *The Scorpion King* we are told that the story takes place in a time before the Pyramids but in this movie, Layla mentions that "everyone should see the pyramids" suggesting that this movie is set long after *The Scorpion King*. Mathayus' companion Ari references both Herodotus (c484BC–c425BC), and Aristophanes of Corinth (c446BC–c386BC) suggesting that the adventure in set nearly two and half millennia after the events seen in the prologue to *The Mummy Returns.*

The historical Sargon of Akkad ruled circa 2334BC– 2279BC.

There is a reference to Gilgamesh entering the Underworld. Historians surmise that Gilgamesh was a Sumerian King who ruled sometime in the period between 2900 – 2350 BC.

Mathayus' brother Jesup does not appear in this movie, the end credits mention a character Jesup, but a deleted scene reveals that this Jesup is one of the party who dies in the underworld.

Notes:

This story bears several similarities to the earlier video game *The Scorpion King: The Rise of the Akkadian*.

The Scorpion King 3: Battle for Redemption

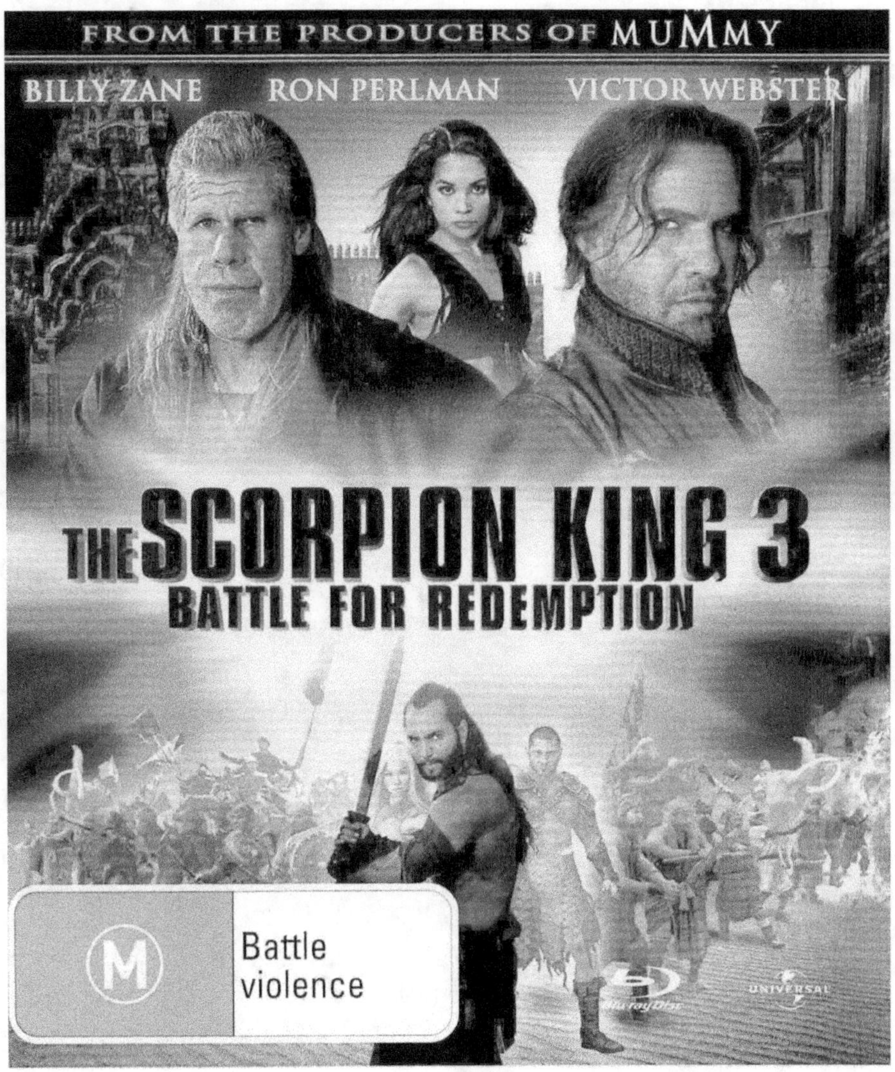

The Scorpion King 3: Battle for Redemption (2012)

Release Date: January 17, 2012

The Cast:

Mathayus The Scorpion King ....Victor Webster

Olaf...Boston Christopher

Silda...Krystal Vee

Argomael......................................Dave Bautista

Zulu Kondo..................................Kevin "Kimbo Slice" Ferguson

Tsukai..Selina Lo

King Horus...................................Ron Perlman

Talus..Billy Zane

King Ramusan...............................Temuera Morrison

Writer: Brendan Cowles and Shane Kuhn (screenplay) Randall McCormick (Story)

Director: Roel Reine

Don't I know you?

Roel Reine – This Dutch director also directed *The Marine 2* (2009), *Death Race 2 and 3* (2010 and 2013), *12 Rounds 2: Reloaded* (2013), and *The Man With the Iron Fists 2* (2015).

Victor Webster – Canadian actor and martial artist also appeared in *Mutant X* (2001-2004) *Continuum* (2012- 2015) and *The Matchmaker Mysteries* (2019 -2021).

Dave Bautista – This former WWE star made a career in Hollywood appearing in *Spectre* (2015), *Stuber* (2019), *Army of the Dead* (2021), *Dune* (2021) as well as Drax in the *Guardians of the Galaxy* series (2014, 2017) and *Avengers: Infinity War* (2018) and *Avengers: Endgame* (2019).

Kevin "Kimbo Slice" Ferguson – A former UFC fighter also appeared in several fight movies *Blood and Bone* (2009), *Circle of Pain* (2010), and *Locked Down* (2010).

Ron Perlman – has nearly 300 credits including *Beauty and the Beast* (1987- 1990) and The *Hellboy* series (2004 and 2008).

Billy Zane – After debuting in *Back to the Future* (1985), he appeared in many movies and TV shows including *The Phantom* (1996), *Titanic* (1997), and *Twin Peaks* (1991).

Temuera Morrison - New Zealand born Morrison came to fame in *Once were Warriors* (1994) he went on to appears as Jango Fett in the *Star Wars* Prequel trilogy and Bobba Fett in *the Manadalorian (2019)* and *the Book of Bobba Fett (2022)*. He also appeared in *Green Lantern* (2011) and *Aquaman* (2018).

Historical Backstory:

None, although the narrator tells us that Prince Talus had been rebelling against his brother King Horus and looting the Far Eastern Kingdom of Horus' ally King Ramusan.

Plot Summary

After the death of Cassandra and the fall of his kingdom – Mathayus renounces the title of Scorpion King and returns to being a mercenary. He is hired by King Horus to go to the aid of his far East ally King Ramusan who is under attack by Horus' brother Talus.

Talus seeks to raise an army to overthrow his brother. Horus mentions that there is an anti-Talus rebel group lead by a leader only known as Cobra. Mathayus is partnered with Olaf, a Teuton from Germania. The pair initially bicker but bond when attacked by a gang of bandits.

They arrive just in time to rescue Ramusan, but war has depleted the kingdom's coffers and Ramusan offers his daughter as a payment instead. Mathayus notices that in a portrait shown by the king, his daughter is wearing the legendary Eye of the Gods amulet and agrees. There is one catch, Princess Silda has been captured by Talus and must be rescued.

Mathayus enters Talus' camp and hires out Olaf to fight for Talus in the battle that is about to start. In the confusion of battle, Mathayus finds Silda, but she is snatched by Cobra's men who manage to escape, leaving behind the Eye of the Gods.

Talus then hires Mathayus and Olaf to find Silda. The pair find Cobra's camp and discover that Silda is Cobra. The pair offer to help Cobra and the resistance and begin training with them.

Talus again attacks Ramusan and this time takes over the castle and obtains the Book of the Dead. With the Eye of the Gods, he reads from the book and summons the three ghost warriors, Zulu Kondo, Argomael and Tsukai

He orders the three spirits to kill all of his men. Then orders Zulu Kondo and Tsukai to search for Cobra's camp and has Argomael stay and guard him.

The two spirits attack the camp, and the resistance warriors battle them. Mathayus finds that his weapons can't injure the spirits. The warriors and Mathayus battle Kondo and defeat him by suspending him off the ground and setting him on fire.

Tsukai returns to Talus, who orders the remaining spirits to guard the Book of the Dead. Tsukai warns that The Scorpion King is near, but Talos is so convinced of his victory that he orders a celebration.

Mathayus and Olaf infiltrate the castle with Silda as prisoner. Talos orders Silda to marry him or be executed and he wants an early wedding night. Mathayus goes to get the medallion and Olaf goes to get the Book of the Dead. Silda distracts Talos to allow Mathayus to enter the room.

Silda sends the signal for Cobra's army to attack as Mathayus tries to steal the medallion. Talus calls for Tsukai and she battles Silda.

Olaf disguised as a guard, searches for the book and gets into a battle with Argomael. Mathayus chases Talus to get the medallion. Talus rides right into the Cobra's army and surrenders the medallion and suggests that he is part of the book now as he is killed by the army.

Olaf and Silda are both defeated but an injured Ramusan and Mathayus have found the Book of the Dead and read the incantation. The spirits offer their allegiance as Ramusan dies.

King Horus and his men arrive to aid in the battle against Talus and find that Mathayus has reclaimed the title of Scorpion King and hands over the wealth of Talus and states that the kingdom no longer accepts Horus' rule.

Horus must decide to give his blessing or blade but states that he respects Mathayus.

Past Lives:

This movie is set after *The Scorpion King* (2002). Mathayus remembers Cassandra (shots of Kelly Hu from the first movie) and we are told that a plague killed The Scorpion King's people and his queen. It is implied that this has recently happened as King Horus states that Mathayus' royal nobility didn't take long to wear off.

However, when Mathayus meets Princess Silda from the Far Eastern Kingdom she states that she had heard the story of how Mathayus became the Scorpion King, it was a tale she heard when she was a little girl. Given that the actress playing Silda was 25, it appears likely that the events recounted in The Scorpion King were at least two decades earlier.

Olaf says that he heard of an Akkadian who was legendary and nearly a god.

Where in the World: King Horus' Kingdom, which appears to Mesopotamian and then moves to King Ramusan's kingdom in the Far East, presumably near present day Thailand.

Bestiary: There is a reference to a blood drinking half-monkey man and Mathayus swears by the Demon Serpent. Olaf reference's Odin's codpiece. King Horus is presumably named for the god of the same name.

Reliquary:

The Book of the Dead and the Eye of the Gods Amulet – when brought together allow the holder to read an incantation releases three warriors from the book:

- Zulu Kondo – The lion spirit from the Land of the Burning Sky
- Argomael
- Tsukai – from the Land of the Rising Sun.

Notes:

It is unclear the Eye of the Gods is needed only to summon and control of the three warriors or if it is needed for all spells in the Book of the Dead. If the latter, this changed sometime in the intervening 5000 years possibly when the lock seen in *The Mummy* and *The Mummy Returns* was added.

Mathayus has a burn on his right arm where the mark of the Black Scorpion was burnt off in *The Scorpion King 2 Rise of a Warrior* but was not present in *The Scorpion King*.

Odin did not appear in the historic record until the Common Era (CE) nearly three thousand years after this adventure.

The Scorpion King 4: Quest for Power

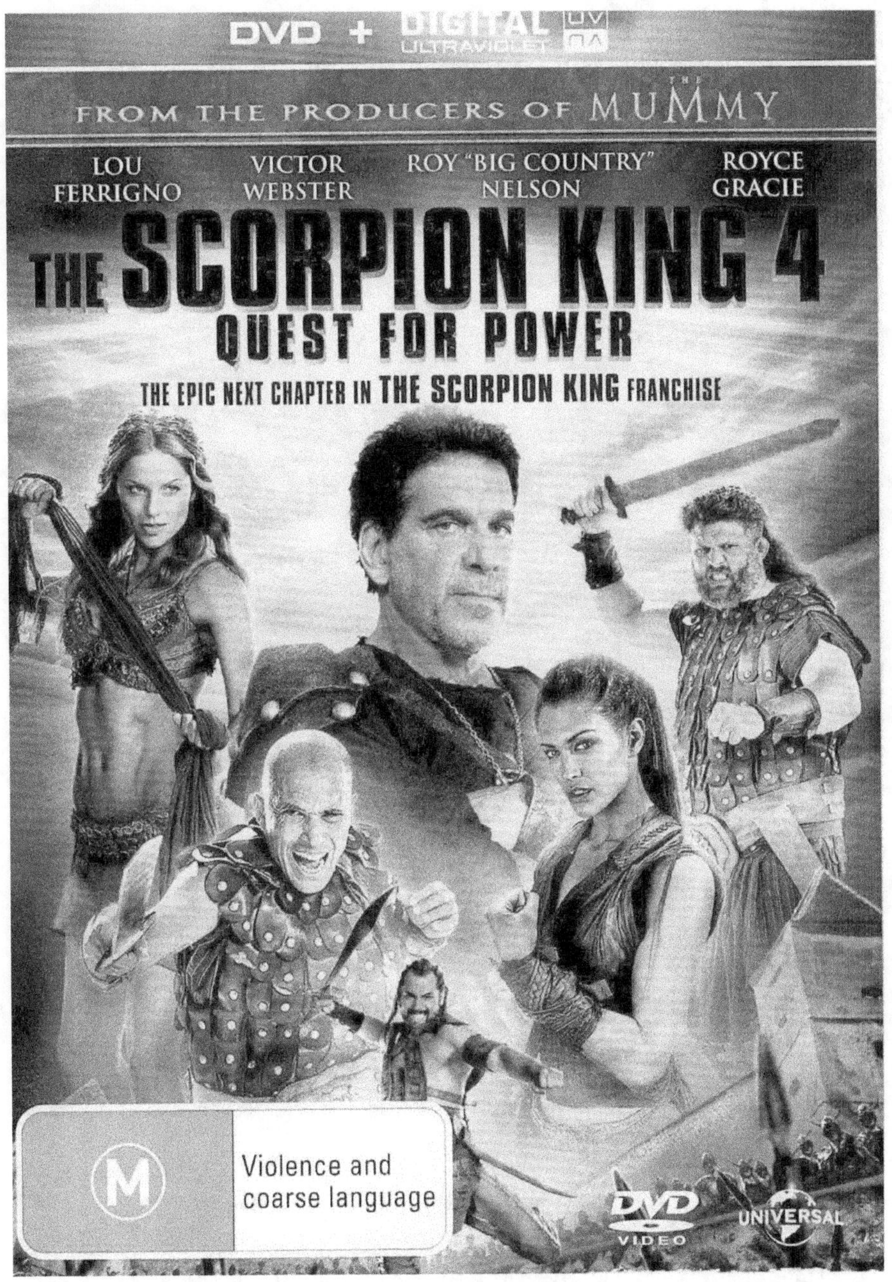

The Scorpion King 4: Quest for Power (2015)

Release Date: January 6, 2015

The Cast:

Mathayus The Scorpion King ....Victor Webster

Valina Reskov.........................Ellen Hollman

Drazen...................................Will Kemp

Sorrell Reskov.......................Barry Bostwick

King Zakkour.........................Rutger Hauer

King Yannick..........................Michael Beihn

Gorak....................................M. Emmett Walsh

Annger ....Royce Grace

Chancara...............................Eve Torres

Skizuma ....Lou Ferrigno

Gizzan..................................Don "The Dragon" Wilson

Roykus.................................Roy "Big Country" Nelson

Cronkus ....Antonio "Bigfoot" Silva

Writer Michael D. Weiss

Director Mike Elliott

Don't I know you?:

Barry Bostwick – Best known as Brad Majors in *The Rocky Horror Picture Show* (1975), he was also the Mayor in *Spin City* (1996-2002).

Rutger Hauer – *Blade Runner* 1982), *Wanted; Dead or Alive* 1986 *Blind Fury* 1989, and *Hobo with a Shotgun* (2011).

Michael Beihn – After playing Kyle Reece in *The Terminator* (1984), he appeared in many TV series and movies including *The Abyss* (1989), *The Magnificent Seven* (1998-2000) and *Adventure Inc* (2002-2003).

Lou Ferrigno – *The Incredible Hulk* (1977-1982) and three reunion movies.

Don "the Dragon" Wilson – Kick boxing champ turned actor appeared in The *Bloodfist* series and the *Ring of Fire* series as well as several other action movies.

Royce Gracie – member of the Gracie family and former UFC fighter.

Eve Torres – former WWE Diva.

Roy "Big Country" Nelson – MMA fighter.

Antonio "Bigfoot" Silva – MMA fighter.

Historical Backstory:

Lord Alcaman, the last king to rule the entire world with magic. He kept his secrets hidden in the Urn of Kings.

Plot Summary:

A camel runs up to a palace dragging its passenger. The guards ask, who did this? The passenger, Drazen, says the most hideous creature, The Scorpion King was responsible. The guards laugh as the Scorpion King is just a campfire story. Mathayus appears behind them and fights and incapacitates the guards.

As Mathayus and Drazen enter the treasure room, they trip the booby traps of multiple spinning blades. After evading the blades, they enter the treasure room to steal the Urn of Kings and set off another booby trap trapping them in a cage. This leads to another battle with the guards and King Skizuma attacks them with his battle axe. Drazen betrays Mathayus and steals the urn.

Mathayus visits his employer King Zakkour who explains the importance of the Urn and sends Mathayus to offer a peace treaty to the Kingdom of Norvania.

Drazen is the son of King Yannick of Norvania and gives his father the Urn of Kings. Yannick breaks the urn to show the key of Lord Alcaman.

Mathayus arrives in Norvania and is arresting trying to see the king. One of his fellow prisoners, is Valina Reskov, of the true royal bloodline.

Drazen tortures Mathayus and Yannick accepts his story of a peace treaty and frees Mathayus. Drazen uses scorpions to kill his father framing Mathayus. Before his death, Yannick hands Mathayus the key of Lord Alcaman.

As Mathayus flees the soldiers, he meets Valina who has broken out of her cell, and they fight off the soldiers. After escaping, the pair make their way to Valina's father's house. Sorrell is an inventor who can treat Mathayus' wound and decipher the Key.

Drazen and his men arrive and burns down Sorrell's house. Drazen follows the clue that Sorrell deciphered.

Mathayus and the Reskovs escape and retrieve the key. The clue reveals that the keyhole is in the temple of the divine Goddess. The men must dress as women to infiltrate the temple. They find the keyhole and it activates a mechanism to show the location of the palace. Drazen is hot on their heels, but they escape to a public house to get a lead on a map to get them past the dragon guarding the forest.

In the public house they find Valina's friend Roland who joins the party. Valina must win a cage fight with Chancara to obtain the map. She wins and the party follows the map to enter the forest. As they camp for the night. Mathayus tells Valina about Cassandra and how she saved him from the poisoned arrow and that it was years ago.

They are captured by the local tribe who unleash multiple large spiders on them. Mathayus yells and the spiders leave them alone, which implies that the Scorpion King can control arachnids. The tribe celebrates and offers guidance on how to get to the palace and tells that the only path there is through the lair of the dragon.

They see the dragon and build a catapult to fight it. Mathayus discovers that dragon is a mechanical device. They head to the mountain and find the secret doorway to the castle.

The castle is full of scientific wonders like magnetic jackets that allows the wearers enhances strength and the ability to fly. They find that Roland has betrayed them has led Drazen straight to the castle. Drazen stabs Sorell. Mathayus must find the crown to heal his friend. He solves the riddles and finds the crown. Drazen follows Mathayus and steals the crown which turns him to ice. Mathayus shatters the ice Drazen.

He then uses the powers of the crown to heal Sorrell and they agree that the secrets of Lord Alcaman are too powerful and hide the palace. With Drazen dead, Sorrell becomes the King of Norvania who abdicates and crowns Valina as the queen.

King Zakkour releases Mathayus from his service and Mathayus becomes the advisor to Queen Valina.

Past Lives:

Drazen has been Mathayus' apprentice for a year.

Where in the World: Al-Moraad, Norvania, Glenrossovia, Tugarin Forest.

Bestiary: Giant spiders, mechanical dragon.

Reliquary: The Urn of Kings, the Key of Lord Alcaman, the Crown of Lord Alcaman.

Notes:

Mathayus looks at Sorrell's catapult with some familiarity as he had been in one during the events of *The Scorpion King*.

The Scorpion King is a legend from over the sands.

Scorpion King: Book of Souls

Scorpion King: Book of Souls (2018)

Release Date: October 23, 2018

The Cast:

Mathayus, the Scorpion King......Zach McGowan

Tala.................................Pearl Thusi

Nebserek.............................Peter Mensah

Amina...............................Katy Louise Saunders

Enkidu.............................Nathan Jones

Khensa.............................Mayling Ng

Chief Uruk.............................Howard Charles

Mensofer (The Seer)................Inge Beckmann

King Tarqa...........................Irshaad Ally

King Memtep........................Tamar Burjaq

Writer David Alton Hedges and Frank De John

Director Don Michael Paul

Don't I know you?:

Don Michael Paul – the writer of *Harley Davidson and the Marlborough Man* (1991) and director of *Tremors* 5 to 7 (2015- 2020).

Zach McGowan – appeared in *Black Sails* (2014-2016) and *Death Race 4: Beyond Anarchy* (2018).

Peter Mensah appeared in *Jason X* (2001), *Spartacus* (2010-2013), *300* (2006) and *300 Rise of an Empire* (2014).

Mayling Ng – appeared in *Wonder Woman* (2017) and *The Suicide Squad* (2021).

Pearl Thusi appeared in *Quantico* (2016-2017), and *Tremors 5: Bloodlines* (2015).

Nathan Jones – former WWE wrestler who appeared in *Troy* (2003), *Conan the Barbarian* (2011) and *Mad Max: Fury Road* (2015).

Historical Backstory:

In Ancient Egypt, before the time of the pharaohs, King Memtep, who is most likely Sumerian, made a deal with Anubis to forge a powerful sword, the Fang of Anubis which takes the souls of all it kills. The names are written in the Book of Souls condemning them to eternal suffering.

Plot Summary

The warlord Nebserek and his loyal army including a priestess rob the tomb of King Memtep and take the Fang of Anubis. Nebserek used the dark magic of the sword and raised a jackal army and have overrun the land. Nebserek is not satisfied, and he sends his men to hunt for the Scorpion King.

Mathayus is living in a village working as a blacksmith. He has given up the life of violence, he gives Abel a young village boy much the same advice as Ashur, being a warrior is not all glory.

Nebserek's lieutenant Khensa attacks the village burning it to the ground. Mathayus fights the intruders, but archers shoot him full of arrows weakening him as Khensa kills Abel before his eyes.

Mathayus is taken prisoner but is rescued by Tala, the daughter of Balthazar. She performs magic over Mathayus and scorpions sting him to give him strength. Tala explains that she needs him to help her find the Book of Souls to defeat Nebserek.

They ride into the valley of the Black Arrows. The tribe take them prisoner Mathayus offers to let them hunt him, if he survives they go free. He fights and defeats the hunters sparing the life of Uruk, their chieftain

Tala and Mathayus enter the Valley the 13 Moons looking for the Temple of Scrolls which according to legend contains the Book of Souls. It can only be entered on the blue moon; Tala uses a cypher scroll with lenses attached to the end of her spear to open the gateway and they enter the Temple of Scrolls.

They are attacked by Enkidu, a golem, but the battle is stopped by his mistress. Amina . As she puts her hand in the moonlight we see writing on her hands and body and we discover that she is the Book of Souls she gains all the knowledge of the souls written on her skin.

Amina tells them that the secret lies in King Memtep's tomb in Amonesh, but she cannot leave the temple as Enkidu won't let her. Using the knowledge that Enkidu fears fire and Tala sets a hallway on fire and they escape taking Amina with them.

Nebserek's men spilt up to cover the two exits from the Valley. Mathayus and Tala battle one of the groups of Nebserek's men as Enkidu following his mistress joins the battle turning the tide.

They make it Aqaba to hire a boat to Amonesh but the second group of Nebserek's men are there also. Mathayus fights them to allow the rest of the party to escape but Tala ignores his instructions to provide a getaway wagon.

Soon the party is on a boat and Amina feels the death of King Tarqa, Tala's brother, by the Fang of Anubis as part of Nebserek's attack on the Nubian people.

The party find the lost city of Amonesh with two pyramids and enter the tomb. They find a stone Androsphinx in the tomb and smash it open and to discover a scroll telling how to stop the Fang of Anubis – the sword must kill Amina. Amina is the daughter of King Memtep and has been alive for centuries.

Nebserek's men captures the party and take them to their leader. The Sand people see the Scorpion King and his party being taken to Nebserek.

The Scorpion King is chained, and his party put into cages. Nebserek decides that he must kill Mathayus in battle and that Amina must be burnt.

Tala summons the scorpions who sting Mathayus giving him strength – he breaks the chains and challenges Nebserek. The Sand People come to the Scorpion King's aid and the Nubian captives rise up as Enkidu smashes the cage and battle the Jackal army. Enkidu is stabbed with the sword and falls into the fire. Mathayus and Nebserek continue to fight with Mathayus throwing Nebserek into the fire killing him. Mathayus walks into the flames and retrieves the fang of Anubis. Amina tells him to break the curse and she walks onto the blade destroying it and herself with a last kiss with Mathayus.

Mathayus rides off alone with a new purpose as the Scorpion King.

Past Lives:

Balthazar has since passed.

Tala has been waiting 56 moons (about 4 and half years) to enter the Valley of the 13 Moons.

Where in the World: Egypt, Sumer.

Bestiary: Enkidu – a golem, Anubis, Amina – the Book of Souls.

Reliquary: The Moon Cypher, The Fang of Anubis, A Lunar Scroll.

The Scorpion King: The Akkadian Prophecy

The Scorpion King: The Akkadian Prophecy Issue 1 (2002)

The Scorpion King: The Akkadian Prophecy Issue 2 (2002)

Release Date: March 2002 and April 2002

Writer: Scott Allie

Artist: Cliff Richards (pencils), Will Conrad (inks)

Publisher: Dark Horse

The Cast:

Mathayus

Jesup

King Telent

Amnakh

Memnon

The Sorcerer

Rah-Nok

Queen Isis

Don't I know you?:

Several characters from the Scorpion King appear or are referenced in this mini-series.

Plot Summary:

Issue 1

Mathayus is hunting, Jesup tells him the King wishes to see him. King Telent would like to be able to predict Memnon's movements and asks Mathayus and Amnakh to ride to the Desert Cataract to obtain the Book of Tehuti, a divine prophetic tool.

Along the way the pair fight demon jackals. They reach the desert cataract and enter the lair of Hro, who is be a monstrous beast with the heads of multiple creatures including a jackal, a crow, a cat, and a rhinoceros beetle. The pair slay Hro and find the book, but not before

Hro warns them the book in the right hands can make a king the ruler of the elements, but that Telent is not the right man.

In the closing scene, Memnon is talking to his sorcerer, who tells him that the Akkadians have the Book of Tehuti.

Issue 2

Telent gets the book but cannot read it and makes his own interpretation.

Memnon decides to send his man Rah-Nok to steal the book.

Meanwhile Queen Isis contacts King Telent to try to get the Akkadians to join an alliance against Memnon but Telent dismisses her and has Mathayus lead his army of five thousand warrior against Memnon.

Telent has left the book behind when Rah-Nok and Memnon's army attack the Akkadians. Rah-Nok slays Amnakh but is avenged by Mathayus.

It appears that Jesup and Mathayus are the only Akkadian survivors.

Past Lives:

Mathayus, in a fit of madness, killed the previous king Trion

Where in the World: The deserts near Gomorrah. (near modern day Jordan).

Bestiary: Demon Jackals. Hro the guardian of the Book of Tehuti.

Reliquary: The Book of Tehuti.

Notes:

Tehuti is another name for Thoth. The Book of Tehuti does bear a resemblance to the Book of Thoth seen in "Orb of Aten" *The Mummy, The Animated Series.*

This miniseries was advertised in the CD insert for *The Scorpion King* Soundtrack.

Ad for The Scorpion King: The Akkadian Prophecy

Ad for The Scorpion King: The Akkadian Prophecy

The Scorpion King: Rise of the Akkadian

The Scorpion King: Rise of the Akkadian PS2 (2002)

Release Date: September 11, 2002

The Cast:

Mathayus.. Dwayne "the Rock" Johnson

Jesup.. Gregg Berger

Rama.. Rino Romano

King Urmhet...................................... Earl Poen

Magus.. Billy West

Hammet.. Daran Norris

Ptah.. Billy West

Apep.. Mark Hamill

Set.. Daran Norris

Producer Jon Sieker

Lead Artist: Ivan Enriquez

Don't I know you?:

Rino Romano the voice of Spiderman in *Spiderman Unlimited* and Batman in *The Batman* Animated series.

Billy West – the voice of Fry, Dr Zoidberg and Professor Farnsworth in *Futurama*, and Skeets in both *Justice League Unlimited* and *Batman: The Brave and the Bold*.

Mark Hamill – Luke Skywalker in the *Star War* series, voice actor including The Joker in *Batman: The Animated series* and spinoffs as well as Chucky in the *Child's Play* reboot.

Plot Summary

The Akkadian people are known assassins, ruled by King Urmhet and Mathayus is taking the test to become an assassin and defeats both Rama and Jesup.

King Urmhet sends Mathayus to assassinate the lord of Kehmet who has murdered one of his concubines. Upon arriving in the city, Mathayus finds that the lord has already been killed and is attacked by Anubis. After Mathayus temporarily vanquishes the god, the wizard Magus reveals himself. Magus wishes for Mathayus to assist him in a spell, but Mathayus refuses and is sent to the dungeon. His cellmate Hammet tells Mathayus that he was a rival to Magus. Mathayus breaks out with Hammet but must battle a sea serpent

Mathayus finds that Magus had attacked his village with Anubis and Horus warriors and killed all but Rama and Jesup. Hammet tells of Osiris' sword used by Set to slay his brother. The sword can be found in the netherworld, and an island to the north has a chamber with the sword guarded by strange beasts.

He travels to Crete but is shipwrecked on the island of Minoa which is being plagued by a minotaur. Mathayus slays the beast and finds himself in the netherworld with Ptah who tells him that he made the sword, but it was shattered by Set's betrayal. If Mathayus can collect all the pieces Ptah can repair it.

Mathayus battles a Sphinx, Bast's warrior and the snake god's warriors collecting the pieces and Ptah reforges the sword warning Mathayus that the sword can be used for good or evil and Mathayus must battle Apep to leave the netherworld.

He frees Hammet who reveals that Magus has captured his brothers Jesup and Rama. Before revealing that Hammet was Magus in disguise all along to trick Mathayus to do his bidding.

Magus uses the sword to summon Set to enslave the world. Mathayus frees himself and kills Magus. This was another trick as Magus' death gives Set a vessel in our world.

Mathayus uses the sword to kill Set and Mathayus and his brothers are the last surviving Akkadians

Where in the World: Akkad.

Bestiary: Anubis, Anubis warriors, Sea serpent, Horus warriors, Minotaur, Androsphinx, Bast Warriors, Apep, and Set.

Reliquary: The Sword of Osiris.

Notes:

This story bears several similarities to the later movie *The Scorpion King 2: Rise of a Warrior.*

The instruction booklet for this game reveals that Rama is the middle brother between Jesup and Mathayus. He is the third surviving Akkadian hired in *The Scorpion King.*

The Scorpion King: Sword of Osiris

The Scorpion King: Sword of Osiris Gameboy (2002)

Release Date: April 2, 2002

The Cast:

Mathayus

Cassandra

Menthu

Isis

Game Concept: Nick Torchia and Sean Krankel

Plot Summary

Cassandra visits a temple where she has received a message to meet Mathayus. She hears him call for help and races to his rescue only to discover that she has been tricked by Menthu and Isis. Isis is covered in markings and riddles, and they want to use Cassandra's gift to solve the riddles to find the Scorpion Stone.

Mathayus arrives at the temple and hears Cassandra's screams and fights his way to her. Cassandra appears as a psychic vision offering guidance to Mathayus. She tells him to find the Sword of Osiris as it is the only thing that can defeat Menthu. She then directs him to the Hero's Gauntlet which is missing the six Runes of Osiris. When the Runes are fused to the gauntlet they can be used to destroy the stone.

Mathayus battles through various creatures and booby traps finding four of the runes of Osiris and the sword of Osiris.

Mathayus arrives just as Menthu, and Isis find the Scorpion Stone. Menthu and Mathayus battle with Mathayus victorious but Isis uses the Scorpion Stone to transform into a half scorpion creature and fights Mathayus. After defeating Isis, Mathayus and Cassandra are reunited and vow to fight evil side by side.

(There is also a version where Isis gets away with the Scorpion Stone. Mathayus and Cassandra are reunited and vow to find the rest of the Runes of Osiris to destroy the Scorpion Stone.)

Where in the World: Egypt.

Bestiary: including mummies, snakes, hyena men, scarabs, Jackal warriors, giant spiders' skeletons, floating skulls, a water elemental skull, pygmy zombies, four-armed warrior women (Kali?), giant eagles, bat people, panthers, eagle men, a demon beetle, and flying head and hands.

Reliquary: The Scorpion Stone, the Heroes Gauntlet, the Runes of Osiris, the Sword of Osiris

Notes:

Isis is not Queen Isis, one of Mathayus' allies in *The Scorpion King*.

The game spells Akkadian as Arcadian.

The instruction booklet tells us that it has been some time since Mathayus defeated Memnon.

Other Miscellaneous Items

"Forever May Not Be Long Enough" by Live

The video clip for the soundtrack for *The Mummy Returns.* It consists of the band Live playing on Egyptian sets. The soundtrack album included the film score by Alan Silvestri.

The Scorpion King Soundtrack - Music from and inspired by the motion picture.

The Scorpion King Soundtrack (2002)

The soundtrack was released on March 22, 2002, just prior to the release of the movie and featured sixteen tracks.

No.	Title	Performer(s)	Length
1.	"I Stand Alone"	Godsmack	4:05
2.	"Set It Off" (Tweaker remix)	P.O.D.	4:10
3.	"Break You"	Drowning Pool	2:48
4.	"Streamline"	System of a Down	3:36
5.	"To Whom It May Concern"	Creed	5:09
6.	"Yanking Out My Heart"	Nickelback	3:35
7.	"Losing My Grip"	Hoobastank	3:55
8.	"Only the Strong"	Flaw	4:17
9.	"Iron Head"	Rob Zombie (featuring Ozzy Osbourne)	4:10
10.	"My Life"	12 Stones	3:03
11.	"Along the Way"	Mushroomhead	3:17
12.	"Breathless"	Lifer	4:04
13.	"Corrected"	Sevendust	4:31
14.	"Burn It Black"	Injected	2:42
15.	"27"	Breaking Point	3:38
16.	"Glow"	Coal Chamber	3:06
Total Run time: 1:00:41			

"I Stand Alone" by Godsmack

The lead track and only single release from the soundtrack of *The Scorpion King,* creates a sequel narrative where Sully Erna, the lead singer of Godsmack, gets a vision of Cassandra. After being bitten by a scorpion, he becomes the new Scorpion King. While the video clip did use clips from the movie, it also filmed new scenes with Dwayne "The Rock" Johnson and Kelly Hu as Mathayus and Cassandra respectively, including a scene where a bed of scorpions turns into Mathayus who later dissolves back into scorpions.

The Revenge of the Mummy Ride

This indoor rollercoaster is a ride at Universal Studios theme parks in Hollywood, Florida, and Singapore. Each one offers a different experience, but all revolve around Imhotep trying to steal the souls of the riders. Imhotep is voiced by Arnold Vosloo.

The Florida version has a behind the scenes video for the making of The Mummy, where the curse of the Mummy has struck several of the cast and crew and features a skeptical Brendan Fraser, who refuses to wear the symbol of the Medjai as protection.

The Hollywood version is set in 1944 during an archeological dig with Omid Djalili reprising his role of the Warden Gad Hassan from *The Mummy* warning riders that the curse is real.

The Singapore version has a voice calling you to find the book of the Amon Ra to end the curse.

Various mummies and other terrors leap out at riders including scarabs.

MTV Parody

Created as the opening to the 2001 MTV movie awards, this skit parodies *The Mummy Returns* with Oded Fehr returning as Ardeth Bay. Hosts Jimmy Fallon and Kirsten Dunst, as themselves take on the Rick and Evy roles, with Snoop Dogg as Izzy and Rob Schneider as Imhotep.

Oded Fehr Cameo Video (2020)

In 2020, Oded created a video on the Cameo platform in character as Ardeth Bay. The video is set in 2020 and features the elderly Medjai in retirement in California. Ardeth says that he is happy in his retirement, devoting time to cooking, where he uses his sword to cut the ingredients, spend time with Horus, a chicken and watching the 2017 *The Mummy* commenting on the fact they put the mummy on a plane.

However when his old friend Rammi calls we discover through subtitles, that Ardeth hates California, everyone thinks he is a rapper and wants to get back to his old life. Rammi ends the call saying that the mummy has returned again.

How Many Scorpion Kings?

There is a disconnect between the villainous Scorpion King seen in the *Mummy Returns* and the heroic version seen in the stand-alone Scorpion King movies. I've seen it claimed on several sites that that Stephen Sommers, who wrote both *The Mummy Returns* and *The Scorpion King* and directed the former, effectively retconned his own movies and claimed the villain seen in *The Mummy Returns* was the look-a-like grandson of the Scorpion King seen in the 2002 movie. There is no source given for this and it is just stated as a fact. I'm not saying that Sommers never said that but in all my research I have not been able to find any evidence that he did.

This got me wondering, is there more than one man named Mathayus who bore the title of the Scorpion King? Certainly, in various royal houses there have been multiple kings of the same name, the English Royal family for example has six kings named George. Indeed, there are two historical King Scorpions who were the inspiration for the Scorpion King. Which leads to the question, are the five actors all playing the same man?

To avoid confusion between the various men who may have been Mathayus, I will be referring to the Scorpion King by surname of the actor playing him.

The Scorpion King media can be divided thusly:

Dwayne Johnson – *The Mummy Returns, The Scorpion King, The Scorpion King: Rise of the Akkadian* (video game), *The Scorpion King: The Sword of Osiris* (video game), and *The Scorpion King: The Akkadian Prophecy* (comic). The last three all use Johnson's likeness for the Scorpion King.

Michael Capon – *The Scorpion King 2: Rise of a Warrior*. Pierre Marias played the younger version of Mathayus in the prologue to this movie while Capon took the role for much of the movie. As it clear that these are the same person, I will refer to this Scorpion King as Capon.

Victor Webster – *The Scorpion King 3: Battle for Redemption* and *The Scorpion King 4: Quest for Power.*

Zach McGowan – *Scorpion King: Book of Souls*

It seems that we, the audience, are expected to assume that the five movies tell the story of the same man. There are references to people and places in the six movies that would certainly suggest this – *The Scorpion King 3: The Battle for Redemption* has Victor Webster recalling his wife Cassandra (Kelly Hu), shown in a clip from *The Scorpion King,* or the fact that in *Scorpion King: Book of Souls,* Tala tells McGowan that she is the daughter of Balthazar from *The Scorpion King.*

However, there is a piece of supplemental material from *The Scorpion King* that throws this into doubt. As part of the promotion for *The Scorpion King* there was a soundtrack album featuring songs from and inspired by the movie. The lead single, which played over the end credits, was "I Stand Alone" by Godsmack.

In the music video, we see Sully Erna, the lead singer, riding through a desert with the rest of the band on his motorcycle. They stop at a petrol station and Sully sees a vision of Cassandra (Kelly Hu) who says that "the prophecy is upon us." Sully is then stung by a scorpion and a tattoo of the scorpion appears on his hand.

Sully then follows an ancient map, shown in flashback to be used by Cassandra, and discovers what appears to be a Scorpion temple. The guardian skeletons bow to him, and Sully gets memory flashes of the Scorpion King, and a nest of scorpions appear and become Dwayne Johnson who passes the sword to Sully. The implication is that Sully is connected to Mathayus and becomes the new Scorpion King. The making of video suggests that Sully is a descendant.

Could this be what happened to Capon, Webster, and McGowan?

There is some evidence to suggest this. In *The Scorpion King* we are told that the story takes place in a time before the Pyramids but in *The Scorpion King 2: The Rise of the Warrior* when Michael Capon was heading to Egypt, Layla, his travelling companion mentions that "everyone should see the pyramids" suggesting that Capon's movie is set long after The Scorpion King. Capon's companion Ari references both Herodotus (c484BC–c425BC), and Aristophanes of Corinth (c446BC–c386BC) suggesting that the adventure in set nearly two and half millennia after the events seen in the prologue to *The Mummy Returns.*

Capon's brothers (Noah and Enki) do not share the name of the brother (Jesup) seen in *The Scorpion King*. (A character named Jesup does appear in the movie he is one of the warriors who joins Capon in the labyrinth and in a deleted scene is shown dying during their adventures in the underworld.)

At the end of *The Scorpion King 2: The Rise of a Warrior*, Capon burns off his scorpion tattoo. Neither Johnson nor McGowan bear a scar on their arms, but Webster does.

In both of Webster's films (*The Scorpion King 3: The Battle for Redemption* and *The Scorpion King 4: Quest for Power*) it is stated that the Scorpion King is a campfire story and legend told to young children implying that there has been some time after the events of *The Scorpion King*.

The only firm date in the story of the Scorpion King is the 3067BC in the opening segment to *The Mummy Returns*. In the Special Features of the *Scorpion King*, we are frequently told that the story takes place in 3000BC – some 67 years after the events seen in *The Mummy Returns*.

In commentary for *The Scorpion King 3: The Battle for Redemption*, the director Roel Reine tell us that it is 4000BC.

In *The Scorpion King 3: The Battle for Redemption*, Webster states that the Scorpion King is dead and buried, and one of the spirits of the Book of the Dead states that The Scorpion King is one of them.

Talos, the villain of *The Scorpion King 3: The Battle for Redemption*, is seen using a telescope with ground lenses – a process that was not invented until the 17th Century, although it was rumored that Emperor Nero (37AD-68AD) may have worn an early type of glasses.

In *Book of Souls* – McGowan is frequently referred to as blacksmith – and one of his enemies refers to giving him a death worthy of A Scorpion King (emphasis mine)

Could it be that there have been several men who have been summoned over the years to bear the spirit or mantle of the Scorpion King? Are the anachronisms a device to hide the fact that we are seeing not the adventures of one man but many?

Ultimately, for the purposes of this book I have decided that Mathayus was one man, but it makes for an intriguing possibility that there may be more than one Scorpion King throughout history. One wonders if the announced Scorpion King reboot set in the modern day may take this option to connect the new film to the original.

An Alternate take on the Scorpion King in The Mummy Returns

We are introduced to the Scorpion King in the opening to *The Mummy Returns*. We are told that in the year 3067BC , The Scorpion King is wearing the bracelet of Anubis, and has formed an army that sought to take over the known world. He trampled kingdoms until he reached Thebes and after a battle lasting seven years he was driven off into the desert. His army died wandering the desert until only he survived. He called upon the god Anubis and gained control of the Army of Anubis to defeat his enemies.

Or so Ardeth Bay tells us, a five-thousand-year-old story. Two full millennia before the formation of the Medjai. Evy O'Connell's research disputes some of the claims made in that opening – her chapter on the Scorpion King formed the opening chapter of *The Mummy Returns* novelization by Max Allan Collins. She tells us that instead of 3067BC it was 3112BC and his campaign only lasted for five years. In the movie itself, Evy tells us that very little is known of the Scorpion King and that he was only a figure of myth with no contemporary writings of his exploits.

What we know of the Scorpion King himself is contradictory and *The Mummy Returns* does not give the Scorpion King a name.

A year later we were given some backstory in the movie *The Scorpion King* about how an Akkadian warrior named Mathayus became The Scorpion King with his sorceress wife Cassandra at his side. Many pointed out that there was a disconnect between the heroic Mathayus as seen in this film and the villainous Scorpion King seen in *The Mummy Returns.*

This disconnect continued through the other appearances of Mathayus. The Scorpion King is portrayed as heroic in the prequels *The Scorpion King 2: Rise of a Warrior* (movie), *Scorpion King: Rise of the Akkadian* (game) and *Scorpion King: The Akkadian Prophecy* (comic). This is to be expected.

In the stories set after *The Scorpion King* (*The Scorpion King: The Sword of Osiris* (game), *The Scorpion King 3: Battle for Redemption*, *The Scorpion King 4: Quest for Power* and *Scorpion King: Book of Souls*) we have seen

Mathayus gain and lose at least three kingdoms and a similar number of queens. Yet we have never seen him act for conquest, his enemies have all sought conquest but not Mathayus.

Some fans suggested that the Scorpion King seen in *The Mummy Returns* was not Mathayus but rather his look-a-like grandson who also took the mantle of the Scorpion King. This is attributed to a quote by Steven Sommers, the writer of both *The Mummy Returns* and *The Scorpion King* but I have never found a source for this.

However, as I watched the fifth and final movie *The Scorpion King: Book of Souls*, I noticed that Mathayus' enemy Nebserek bears many similarities to Scorpion King as seen in *The Mummy Returns*. Nebserek is a tyrant trying to conquer the known world with an artefact connected to the god Anubis. He has amassed an army referred to as Jackals. Certainly, it would not be impossible over thousands of years of retellings that that battle between Nebserek and Mathayus, the Scorpion King would become garbled, and the hero became conflated or confused with the villain. The story of a jackal army made up of human soldiers, growing in the telling to become literal jackal-headed demons ravaging the land.

There is a flaw in this theory- the existence of the Bracelet of Anubis in 1933. This artefact, aside from the connection to Anubis, bears no resemblance or connection the sword known as the Fang of Anubis, which was destroyed along with the titular Book of Souls at the end of *The Scorpion King: Book of Souls*.

However, it makes for an interesting thought that the tales of Mathayus and Nebserek were confused and intertwined in the intervening millennia.

The Kings of Akkad

Little is known of the first kingdom of Akkad, which predates the more famous empire of the same name by nearly a millennium. What little we know of the Kingdom and its rulers come from the early life of the Akkadian; Mathayus later known as the Scorpion King. While not an Akkadian king, Mathayus interacted with the last six kings of Akkad.

The kingdom is in a fertile valley where nomadic tribes stopped their wandering training to be assassins. The boundaries of the first Akkadian kingdom appear to be similar to the later Akkadian Empire, between the Tigris and the Euphrates rivers, with the capital being in the city of Nippur as seen in *The Scorpion King 2: Rise of Warrior.*

The Akkadian empire had existed for generations before the birth of Mathayus and their elite warriors the Black Scorpions were prized as the bodyguards of kings and princes.

Hammurabi (????-3118BC?) – The earliest known King of Akkad. Little is known of him but when Hammurabi came upon Ashur, father of Mathayus, and his general Sargon battled over Mathayus' participation in the games to select the next group of recruits for the Black Scorpions, he stopped the fight and pardoned Ashur and insisted that Mathayus be trained as a Black Scorpion against his father's wishes. Shortly after Hammurabi died. The official report was the Hammurabi died in an accident, but it was widely rumored that he was killed by Sargon. (*The Scorpion King 2: Rise of Warrior*)

Sargon (3118BC?-3112BC?) – Originally the commander of the Akkadian armies. While Mathayus was away undertaking his Black Scorpion training, it was reported that Sargon had slain Hammurabi and seized the throne for himself. The king sought to stamp out such rumors and ordered Mathayus to slay his brother Noah who was charged with slandering the king's name. Sargon was a practitioner of black arts worshipping Astarte and used his magic to slay his rivals and enemies. Sargon makes a deal for more power by sacrificing all his subjects. Mathayus' allies prevented this. Sargon died in battle with Mathayus. (*The Scorpion King 2: Rise of Warrior*)

Shalmaneser (3112BC? –????) –The son of Hammurabi, who claimed the throne of Akkad after the death of Sargon. Mathayus' companion Layla suggested that as the one who slew Sargon, Mathayus should have been new king, but he did not want that. (*The Scorpion King 2: Rise of Warrior*)

Trion – (????–????) – little is known of this King, and it is unclear if he is related to Shalmaneser. In a fit of madness, Mathayus slew Trion. His death allowed his brother Telent to claim the throne. (*The Scorpion King: The Akkadian Prophecy*)

Telent – ???? – 3107BC) – Telent rose to the throne after the death of his brother Trion and gained control of the five thousand strong Akkadian army. He was king when Memnon seized control of Gomorrah. Jealous of Memnon's sorcerer, he ordered Mathayus and Amnakh to find the Book of Tehuti, a divine prophetic tool. Telent is unable to correctly interpret the pages of the book and predicts his own victory. He refuses the offer of Queen Isis to form an alliance with her and King Pheron to battle Memnon, instead trusting his flawed prophecy. Telent lead his army into battle and is ambushed by Memnon's superior army and most of his army is killed. (*The Scorpion King: The Akkadian Prophecy*)

Urmhet (3107BC–3102BC) – the last King of Akkad, presumably succeeded Telent after the latter's death in 3107BC. After the military defeat of the Akkadians under the leadership of Telent, it appears that Urmhet disbanded the Akkadian army and focused on individual assassins, possibly on the hopes that Memnon might leave Akkad alone. Urmhet is a fair king, taking on cases of injustice, he sends Mathayus to dispense a town lord who murdered one of his concubines. However, this is all a plot to manipulate Mathayus into assisting the sorcerer Magus. When Mathayus refuses, Magus attacks Akkad killing all but Mathayus, Jesup and Rama. This attack and the death of Urmhet brings the end of the first Akkadian empire. (*The Scorpion King: Rise of the Akkadian*)

The Great Alex O'Connell Time Discrepancy

Alex O'Connell first appeared in *The Mummy Returns*, the 2001 sequel to the 1999 *Mummy* reboot film as the child of Rick O'Connell and Evelyn nee Carnahan.

The O'Connell's timeline in *The Mummy* and *The Mummy Returns* runs as follows:

THE MUMMY

1923 (date on screen) – Rick O'Connell and his Foreign Legionnaire Battalion discover Hamunaptra. All Legionnaires except Rick and his colleague Beni die.

Three Years Later (text on screen) - 1926 Evelyn Carnahan and her brother Jonathan meet Rick and hire him to take them to Hamunaptra.

THE MUMMY RETURNS

1933 – Rick and Evelyn have married and have a son Alex. At one point, Alex states that he is only eight years old.

This last fact creates a problem, for Alex to be eight he must be born in either 1925 (7 turning 8) or 1924 (8 turning 9), which means that he must be born at least a year prior to the date given for his parents meeting.

This leaves the chronologist searching for a solution to this conundrum. I have identified three possible solutions:

1. Alex's age is wrong.
2. the dates given for these two adventures are wrong, or
3. Alex is not the biological child of Rick and Evelyn O'Connell.

ALEX'S AGE IS WRONG

After the release of *The Mummy Returns* there are several other recorded adventures of Alex O'Connell:

- *The Mummy The Animated series* (2 seasons),
- *The Mummy Chronicles* (4 Books),
- *The Mummy: The Rise and Fall of Xango's Ax* (4 issue comic miniseries), and

- the 2008 movie *The Mummy: Tomb of the Dragon Emperor.*

The Animated series, and Xango's Ax offer no guidance in this debate either not giving Alex's age or the year of the adventures in the actual adventures.

The Mummy: Tomb of the Dragon Emperor is set in early 1947 (Chinese New Year) but does not give us Alex's age. However, secondary material, *The Mummy Tomb of the Dragon Emperor: A Newmarket Pictorial Moviebook* states that during script development Alex's age was changed from 17 to 21. If the moviebook is accurate, this would mean that Alex was born in 1925 as it was unlikely that he had his birthday so early in the year.

The Mummy Chronicles books, on the other hand, offers both the date of the adventure and Alex's age which helps us set the year of birth for Alex O'Connell. The first book opens in 1937 and clearly states that we are four years after the events of The Mummy Returns and Alex is 12. The final book is set in 1938 and Alex is still 12 inferring that he is turning 13 in that year – confirming that he was born in 1925.

We can make further deductions as the first book is set in 1937 and is three months before the second book, which is set in November 1937, making it set in August of that year.

The fourth book takes place in high Summer, as the Egyptian summer begins in June then it is likely that it is set in late July of that year as Alex is still 12 he has not yet had his 13th birthday making his month of birth either July or August.

To make Alex's age align with a 1927 birthdate – either this moves the events to 1935 for the Mummy Returns and 1939/1940 for the Mummy Chronicles books but there is no reference to World War II in those novels – the Italian and German Embassies in Cairo are still open, or Alex is only 6 years old during the events of *The Mummy Returns* and 10 for *The Mummy Chronicles*. This would make Alex 18 turning 19 at the time of *The Mummy: Tomb of the Dragon Emperor.*

ARE THE DATES GIVEN FOR THE MUMMY INCORRECT?

Given that the dates given for *The Mummy Returns* and *The Mummy Chronicles* match up well and moving them later would lead to placing adventures during World War II it is unlikely that those dates are incorrect.

So, are the dates in *The Mummy* correct? Interestingly the Annual for The Animated Series retells the events of the first two movies and retells the first three episodes of the series. It gives the dates as *The Mummy* (1925), *The Mummy Returns* (1935) and that Alex is 11 in the first episode of the Animated Series.

Max Allan Collins' novelization of *The Mummy* sets the 1923 portion of the film in 1925 and the rest of the film takes place "a month and two days later" (p42) instead of 3 years later.

Could the three years later instead be a reference to three months later instead? That would solve that Alex being born prior to his parents meeting but it creates other issues.

In the later Mummy Novelizations of *The Mummy Returns* and *The Mummy: Tomb of the Dragon Emperor*, Collins tells us that Evelyn served as the curator of Cairo Museum from 1925 to 1927 when she left the role to start a family.

The unfinished comic series *The Mummy: Valley of the Gods* is set in 1927 – Rick and Evelyn are on their extended honeymoon with no hint of a child. Jonathan asks when they will be starting a family and Rick replied that they haven't even been married two months. Based on the unpublished scripts for that series, the final scene has Evy being checked by a doctor and announcing that she is pregnant.

However, *The Mummy Returns* novelization, there are multiple references to the events of the first film being a decade earlier in 1923. The movie itself has a similar reference after Red and his men steal the chest.

Ultimately, changing the onscreen dates creates more problems for the chronologist than it solves. Placing the events of *The Mummy* in 1923 is too close to the death of Lord and Lady Carnahan and contradicts evidence from *The Mummy: The Animated series* that Evy graduated from Oxford in 1924.

The 1925 placement is better in that regard but if as Collins says that the Battle of Hamunaptra took place just over a month before the main events of the movie. The earliest possible placement for the legionnaire battle is early January, with the remainder of the movie taking place in February 1925.

We then must move *The Mummy: The Valley of the Gods* to 1925, which is set less than two months after Rick and Evy's wedding. Assuming that the couple married right after the events of *The Mummy*, the earliest this could take place is mid-March (assuming they have been married for five weeks), which is only five months before the birth of Alex in late July/early August in that same year and in 1925 it is highly unlikely that a baby born that premature would survive.

Therefore, the dates given on screen in The Mummy must be correct.

ALEX ISN'T THE SON OF RICK AND EVELYN O'CONNELL

The only conclusion is that Alex O'Connell is not the son of Evy and Rick O'Connell, born in 1925 and adopted by the couple in 1927.

If that is the case, who might be Alex's biological parents?

a) Unknown parents, Alex was found in 1927 as an orphan and adopted by the O'Connells.

b) Someone known by the O'Connells – the O'Connells encountered many people in their recorded and unrecorded adventures, some like Winston Havlock, Beni, Professor Terrence Bey and the American party all died during the 1926 adventure and the O'Connells may have searched for a child and adopted them.

c) Jonathan Carnahan – the idea that Jonathan had a child out of wedlock and his sister adopted the child is certainly possible.

d) Rick O'Connell – there is a three-year period from 1923 when Rick stumbles out of Hamunaptra and 1926 where he met Jonathan in a bar. It's possible that during that time Rick fathered a child and the mother found Rick in 1927. The mother may have been ill and Evy and Rick adopted the boy. In *The Mummy Returns*, Rick's friend Izzy tells a tale of a bank job in Marrakesh where Izzy gets shot and Rick rides off with a belly-dancer. Rick points out that it was before he met Evy and quickly changes the subject. Could the belly dancer be Alex's mother?

Ultimately, with no new material being released in this series we may never know.

There is some circumstantial evidence leaning to option D. In *The Mummy: Tomb of the Dragon Emperor*, Roger Wilson tells Alex that as he was riding into the dig he thought he was looking at Rick. There is a more conclusive piece of evidence for this, in *The Mummy: The Animated Series* episode "Howl," we are told that werewolves attack those of their bloodline and Rick, as a werewolf, attacks Alex.

Did the O'Connells have another child?

In the unpublished finale of *The Mummy: Valley of the Gods*, set in 1927, it is revealed that Evy is pregnant.

While the reader is to assume that this is intended to be Alex O'Connell, it has been shown that Alex was born in July or August 1925 to unnamed woman and Rick O'Connell. So, what came of this pregnancy? Was there another O'Connell child, two years younger than Alex? What can we tell about this child, assuming that it was born?

In *The Mummy: Tomb of the Dragon Emperor,* when Rick and Evy meet Roger Wilson, Wilson declares that Alex is like the son he never had, which Rick replies "and he's the only one we've got." So, it appears that the child was a daughter.

Why do we never see this daughter? It cannot be that as Mr. Chamberlin, The Egyptologist in *The Mummy* expressed, that women were unsuited to adventures or intellectual pursuits. Evy certainly would not hold with those views and would want to have her daughter at her side.

During *The Mummy Returns,* eight-year-old Alex joins his parents on a dig. There is no sign or reference to a younger sibling. While not stated, this might be Alex's first dig so a younger sibling would not be joining them and for the sake of streamlining the plot any reference to this child may have been excised.

When we next see the O'Connells it is during the events of *The Mummy The Animated Series* which is set three years later when Alex is eleven and the sibling would be nine, old enough to attend digs and old enough to join the family on vacation in Scotland as seen in "The Summoning."

In several episodes, Alex is shown to be lonely, unable to make friends as the O'Connell party is racing around the world trying to find the Scrolls of Thebes. However, the family is frequently in Egypt and makes several visits to England – surely Rick and Evy would have had their other child join them at some point?

However, there is a possibility that this second child, was excised from the story to protect them. At the period covered in *The Mummy:*

The Animated Series, The Mummy Chronicles and *The Mummy: Secrets of the Medjai, (1936-1939)* the family was constantly battling supernatural menaces, most often Imhotep and Colin Weasler. The Mummy and his human accomplice were ruthless and would not have hesitated to kidnap and use the weakest and youngest member of the family as leverage against the O'Connells.

After the outbreak of World War II in 1939, we are told in the novelization of *The Mummy Tomb of the Dragon Emperor* that Alex was sent to a boarding school in Australia and a similar arrangement may have been made for his sister.

The child may have been hidden with relatives. In *The Mummy: The Secrets of the Medjai* "A Fair to Remember," Jonathan makes a reference to an Uncle Reginald, presumably the brother of Howard Carnahan, who may have taken custody of the child.

We do have one piece of evidence that might point to the existence of this hidden daughter, but it is not in the any of the works of the Mummy franchise but rather in another of the films of writer director Stephen Sommers and actor Brendan Fraser.

In the 2009 film *G.I. Joe: The Rise of Cobra*, Brendan Fraser appears in a small cameo role as Sergeant Stone. The character was an original creation for the film and in an interview with Fred Topel "Brendan Fraser Geeks Out Over *G.I. Joe* Cameo" Fraser said of his role "I made a personal choice when I arrived and kind of ripped it off and decided I'd be some sort of hybrid of a great-great-grandson of Rick O'Connell" and a similar statement in an interview with MTV "Maybe I could be Rick O'Connell's great-great-grandson".

As part of the tie-in toy line for G.I. Joe: The Rise of Cobra, a Sgt Stone figure was released with a file card that states that Stone is a trainer for the G.I. Joe team and that his full name is Geoffrey Stone IV. This would suggest that his paternal great grandfather was also named Geoffrey Stone. Could it be that Geoffrey Stone I married the daughter of Rick and Evy? It is equally possible that Geoffrey II or Geoffrey III married a daughter or granddaughter of Alex O'Connell.

Of course, this speculation assumes that Evy did carry her 1927 pregnancy to term and had a second child, but we have no evidence of that, and Alex may be an only child.

Was Jonathan a veteran of the Great War?

In the article "Celebrating the chaotic energy of *The Mummy*" by Leah Schnelbach, there is reference to the fan theory that Jonathan has Post Traumatic Stress Disorder (PTSD), as we now call it, from his service in the Great War (World War I).

Certainly, given the period it makes perfect sense. In Max Allan Collins' novelization of *The Mummy*, it is revealed the Jonathan is thirty years old making him born in 1896. At the outbreak of the Great War in 1914 he would have been 18, old enough to legally join one of the armed forces. Certainly, many young men of his age and younger did just that. Is there any evidence that Jonathan was one of them?

Jonathan Carnahan appeared in the three Mummy movies, the animated series and in the *Valley of the Gods* comic. What do we know about Jonathan's background?

Like Evy, he is the child of Howard Carnahan and his Egyptian wife. He was educated in England and in Europe – in *The Mummy The Animated Series* episode "Fear Itself" we are told that Jonathan attended many Universities in Europe because he was constantly being expelled (or as he tells it he had learnt all that he could and was moving on). There are no dates given for his university education, but it is highly unlikely that Jonathan was moving from University to University in Europe during the Great War.

In "A Fair to Remember," he mentions that he was fellow student with Charlie Royce, who he set up on a date with Evy – presumably all three were at the same university, Oxford. However, Charlie mentions that he was the class of 28, which would imply that he enrolled in 1924 for a four-year degree. (Given that Evy was a contemporary and when introduced in *The Mummy* in 1926 it is obvious that she had been working at the Cairo Museum for some time. Therefore, the latest she could have graduated was 1924.)

There are hints that Jonathan served in the Great War. When Jonathan is introduced in *The Mummy*, he is in a sarcophagus using the body inside to scare his sister. She chides him asking if he has no respect for the dead to which he responds, "There are times when I'd rather like to join them." This is very similar to how Winston Havlock, a veteran of the

Great War, desired to go down in a blaze of glory like the "other laddies." Or it may simply be a morbid streak.

At Hamunaptra when Beni points out that the odds are fifteen to four, Rick states "I've had worse." And much to Rick's surprise, Jonathan states "Yeah, me too." There is no explanation of what that situation might be. Given what we have seen of Jonathan it may simply be a reference to a time several of his creditors appeared at the same time asking for money. However, a battle during the Great War is also possible.

In *The Mummy Returns* when asked if he can use a rifle, Jonathan refers to being three-time fox and hound champion. This would seem to be a reference to fox hunting. Surely Jonathan would have referenced his service in the Great War at this point?

In all the adventures, there are very few references to the Great War or events during that period. One half the of the Orb of Aten was discovered in 1916 by an American dig and Winston Havlock served in the Great War. We don't know if Rick lied about his age to enlist, we may presume that Ardeth Bay would have fought as an irregular. Jonathan's war service is another mystery that without further information we cannot solve.

What we know about The Mummy 4

The end of *The Mummy: Tomb of the Dragon Emperor* has a sequel hook where Jonathan Carnahan left China with the Eye of Shangri-La heading for "someplace where they don't have mummies" and he was heading for Peru. This was followed with a note on screen that "Soon after, mummies were found in Peru." This sets the stage for a fourth movie set in Peru.

In an interview with MTV, director Rob Cohen revealed some potential details that the setting was likely to be either Peru or Mexico "If we want to go to Mexico or we want to go to Peru, we can because there's a cultural truth there of the mummies and these beautiful cultures."

Additionally, the Eye of Shangri-La would play a part, Cohen said that the "artifact still having a lot of prizes in it." Presumably, this would imply that the diamond had other powers.

Cohen's third and final hint was that "Rick is now immortal. I'd love to explore how that plays out for him."

We can presume that both Brendan Fraser and John Hanna would be returning for the fourth film. Contemporary interviews with both Maria Bello and Luke Ford had both stating that they had signed on for another three films.

In the aftermath of the failure to launch of the Dark Universe with The Mummy (2017) there have been several articles on sites like Cinemablend, Stanford Arts Review, and Screen Rant discussing what would have happened in the Mummy 4. They point out that film was to be titled *The Mummy: The Rise of the Aztec* (or *Rise of the Aztecs*) and would have had Antonio Banderas as the Aztec Mummy villain, but none of these articles refer to sources for this.

I found an article published on October 30, 2010, by Adam Spinks "THE MUMMY 3 star says THE MUMMY 4 is happening" saying that the rumored title for the fourth film was The Mummy 4: Rise of the Aztec.

There was also a Facebook movie page "*The Mummy: Rise of the Aztec*" created on January 2, 2010, which linked to a now defunct wordpress site "The Mummy: Rise of the Aztec" by VolleyballFreak101. In the only archived post "Do YOU want a 4th Mummy Movie?", dated November 13, 2010, Volleyball Freak stated that the Facebook page was theirs and that there was a rumor that the fourth movie is to be called "*The Mummy: Rise of the Aztec*".

The Facebook page links to Theiapolis, an online movie message board, to a post by "urban legend" on August 18, 2008, titled "The Fourth Mummy Movie Planned" which states, "After Egypt and China Rick O'Connell (Brendan Fraser), Evelyn Carnahan (Maria Bello) and Jonathan (John Hannah) could visit South America in a promising "Rise of the Aztec" episode, scheduled for summer 2010." This may be the source of the Rise of the Aztec subtitle; in any case this title has been adopted throughout the fandom.

As to rumor that Antonio Banderas was involved in this movie, I cannot find any official source for this. There are no articles in the entertainment news sites like Variety or the Hollywood Reporter stating that Banderas was being considered or approached for the role. I did find a user created cast list on imbd.com created by user izzy–Imperiocash20 on January 5, 2013, that had Antonio Banderas listed as Imperio The Aztec Mummy. This cast list matched an entry on Rickipedia with a detailed plotline created on November 25, 2013.

The Mummy / Scorpion King Timeline

Notes on the timeline:

For this timeline, I rewatched and reread everything in the Mummy and Scorpion King franchises. As there were so many different sources, I had to create a hierarchy of authority and came up with the following.

A. The movies
B. *The Mummy Chronicles* books
C. The animated series
D. The comics
E. Original video games, and
F. Novelizations and other adaptations.

Details for that don't directly contradict the movies were included in this timeline.

A primary example of a contradiction is that the Mummy novelization states that the battle of Hamunaptra and the subsequent plot of the movie all took place in 1925 but the movie shows the battle taking place in 1923 and the rest of the movie in 1926. So, for this timeline, I am following the dates shown in the movie.

The Scorpion King franchise provided a challenge as there were no dates provided in the movies, I have made my own estimated dates and shown this by placing an e after the date.

Dates given in the Adventures are given in bold

The series made use of the names of several historical figures, e.g., *The Scorpion King 2: Rise of a Warrior* featured Sargon of Akkad (who ruled c2334BC-c2279BC),and referenced both Herodotus (c484BC-c425BC), and Aristophanes of Corinth (c446BC-c386BC), however the dates of these historical figures do not align with the date given in *The*

Mummy Returns of 3067BC. I have assumed that there was more than one person of that name who had faded into obscurity by the time that the later and better-known bearer of the name came to fame.

Of course, these franchises are not known for their historical accuracy.

I have operated on the assumption that all five Scorpion King movies feature the same man seen in *The Mummy Returns* despite the constant changing of actors.

The Timeline

3131BC (e)

The Birth of Mathayus to Assur and Inanna and will have two younger brothers Enki and Noah. (*The Scorpion King 2: Rise of a Warrior*) Mathayus has an older half-brother Jesup from his mother (*The Scorpion King*). There is another older brother Rama (*The Scorpion King: Rise of the Akkadian*).

3118BC(e)

Scorpion King 2: Rise of a Warrior (movie) – Prologue Mathayus is 13 and leaves for training as a Black Scorpion Warrior.

The death of Assur from Sargon's magic.

3118BC–3112BC(e)

At some point during this time Sargon deposes King Hammurabi and installs himself as king. Given the statues of Sargon that are seen when Mathayus returns it is likely that this took place early in this period. (*Scorpion King: Rise of a Warrior* movie).

6 years later

3112BC(e)

The Scorpion King 2: Rise of a Warrior (movie) Mathayus is 19.

3107BC(e)

The Scorpion King: The Akkadian Prophecy (comic).

3102BC(e)

The Scorpion King: The Rise of the Akkadian (game).

The death of all Akkadians except Mathayus, Jesup and Rama.

3101BC(e)

The Scorpion King (movie).

The death of Jesup and Rama. Mathayus becomes the Scorpion King.

3089BC(e)

The Scorpion King: The Sword of Osiris (game).

Before 3081BC(e)

A plague hits Mathayus' kingdom and wipes out most of his subjects including his wife Cassandra. From the dialog it is implied that this happened recently.

3081BC(e)

The Scorpion King 3: The Battle for Redemption (movie).

3078BC(e)

The Scorpion King 4: Quest for Power (movie).

3075BC(e)

Scorpion King: Book of Souls (movie)

Mathayus meets Tala daughter of Balthazar from *The Scorpion King*.

(Pearl Thusi who plays Tala was 30 at the time of filming).

3067 BC

The Mummy Returns (movie) – Prologue.

3062BC (e)

The Mummy Chronicles: The Curse of the Nile (book) Prologue.

Eleventh Dynasty Sometime between 2130BC-1991BC

The Mummy: Valley of the Gods 1 (comic) Prologue.

1291BC(e)

The time travel parts of "Time Before Time"

However due to nature of time travel, these parts happened and didn't happen.

1290BC

The Mummy (movie) Prologue

Imhotep steals the Book of the Dead to resurrect Anck-Su-Namun.

At the same time, he is also attempting to steal the Scrolls of Thebes and the Manacle of Osiris. (*The Mummy: The Animated Series* (TV)).

331BC

Alexander the Great founds Alexandria.

326BC

Alexander leaves Alexandria, it around this time that he borrows the Scrolls of Thebes. .(Reference in "A Candle in the Darkness" *The Mummy: The Animated Series* (TV)).

200BC

Tomb of the Dragon Emperor (movie) Prologue.

(date given in *The Mummy Tomb of the Dragon Emperor* by Max Allan Collins)

31BC

The Mummy Chronicles: Heart of the Pharoah (movie) – Prologue. The deaths of Marc Anthony and Cleopatra.

Unknown date between 12th century to 15th century

Xango, God of Thunder rules the Oyo Empire in Africa.

(historical records are unclear when Xango ruled. *The Rise and Fall of Xango's Ax* (comic))

1206-1227

The reign of Genghis Khan – it is during this time he acquires a fragment of the Scrolls of Thebes. (Reference in "Fear Itself" *The Mummy: The Animated Series* (TV))

1271

Marco Polo begins his journey to China – he is reported to have the Scrolls of Thebes. (Reference in "The Boy Who Would be King" *The Mummy: The Animated Series* (TV))

1275

Marco Polo meets Kublai Khan and reportedly gifts him the Scrolls of Thebes. (Reference in "The Boy who Would be King" *The Mummy: The Animated Series* (TV))

1529-1541

Francisco Pizarro leads the Spanish conquest of Peru – it is rumored that he carried the Scrolls of Thebes. (Reference in "The Cloud People" *The Mummy: The Animated Series* (TV))

1768-1770

Captain James Cook begins his exploration of the Pacific Ocean including the mapping of the east coast of what is now known as Australia. He was rumored to be carrying the Scrolls of Thebes. (Reference in "Eruption" *The Mummy: The Animated Series* (TV))

1798-1799

Napoleon Bonaparte leads an expedition to Egypt; he discovers the Scrolls of Thebes and takes them to Paris. (Reference in "The Maze" *The Mummy: The Animated Series* (TV))

1876(e)

Sir Colin Bembridge goes missing searching for the Tomb of the Dragon Emperor. Reference in *The Mummy: The Tomb of the Dragon Emperor* (movie).

1896(e)

Jonathan Carnahan is born.

(*The Mummy* novelization states that Jonathan is 30 but looks 40)

1902(e)

Rick O'Connell is born in Chicago to Jack O'Connell and his wife.

(In *The Mummy: The Tomb of the Dragon Emperor* novelization, Rick says he was 20 or so when he was received his battlefield promotion in Hamunaptra in the French Foreign Legion.)

The Mummy novelization states that Rick is from Chicago.

Year from Rickipedia

1903(e)

Evelyn Carnahan is born.

(date from Rickipedia)

1912(e)

Jack O'Connell leaves his wife after being marked as a Medjai and Rick becomes an orphan being placed in orphanages around the world including St Mary's Industrial School for Boys in Baltimore, and Cairo. It is in Cairo where he receives a Medjai tattoo (one wonders of this was it was at the behest of his father).

1916

Half of the Orb of Aten was found in Biyala. (Reference in "Orb of Aten" *The Mummy: The Animated Series* (TV))

1921(e)

Rick was silver mining in Peru. (Reference in "People in the Clouds" *The Mummy: The Animated Series* (TV))

1921(e)

Rick joins the Foreign Legion while drunk in Paris trying to impress a woman.

Reference in *The Mummy* novelization.

1922

Howard Carnahan is present at the discovery of Tutankhamen.

(Both he and his wife die shortly after in a plane crash attributed to the curse.)

Reference in *The Mummy* novelization.

1923

'Ricochet' O'Connell meets Mad Dog Maguire in the French Foreign Legion. (reference in *The Mummy: Tomb of the Dragon Emperor*).

The Mummy Prologue.

Rick O'Connell and his Foreign Legion battalion desert and march to Hamunaptra.

1924(e)

Jonathan sets Evy up on a date with Charlie Royce. (Reference in "A Fair to Remember" *The Mummy: The Animated Series* (TV)).

July or August 1925

Alex O'Connell born.

1925 – 1927

Evelyn Carnahan is working for the Cairo Museum. (It was reported that she left the role to raise a family with her husband Rick O'Connell). The novelizations of *The Mummy* and *The Mummy Returns* incorrectly identify Evy as the curator for the entirety of this period but it is more likely that the promotion to curator took place after the death of the previous curator, Dr Terrence Bey, during the events of *The Mummy*. Interestingly Dr Bey replaced Howard Carnahan after his death.

1926

The Mummy (movie).

1927

The Mummy: Valley of the Gods (comic).

1928

At age 3 Rick and Evelyn take Alex on a picnic near the Sphinx. (reference in *Revenge of the Scorpion King* (book)).

1930

The publication of *The Curse of the Pharaohs: Myth and Mystery* by Dr Evelyn O'Connell.

Reference in *The Mummy Returns* Novelization.

1933

The Mummy Returns (movie).

February 1936(e)

The Mummy: The Animated series "The Summoning"

March 1936(e)

The Mummy: The Animated series "A Candle in the Darkness"

April 1936(e)

The Mummy: The Animated series "Against the Elements"

May 1936(e)

The Mummy: The Animated series "The Deep Blue Sea"

Jun 1936(e)

The Mummy: The Animated series "Orb of Aten"

July 1936(e)

The Mummy: The Animated series "Eruption"

The O'Connells were on their way to Australia prior to the events of this episode. A period must be allowed for them to follow the path of Captain Cook.

Oct 1936(e)

The Mummy: The Animated series "The Black Forest"

Nov 1936(e)

The Mummy: The Animated series "The Cloud People"

Dec 1936(e)

The Mummy: The Animated series "Fear itself"

Feb 1937(e)

The Mummy: The Animated series "The Boy who would be King"

Mar 1937(e)

The Mummy: The Animated series "Howl"

May 1937(e)

The Mummy: The Animated series "The Puzzle"

Jun 1937(e)

The Mummy: The Animated series "The Maze"

Prior to 1937 – Rick O'Connell encounters Zorin Ungricht in a temple in India. (references in Revenge of the Scorpion King and Heart of the Pharaoh (books))

August 1937

The Mummy Chronicles: Revenge of the Scorpion King

October/November 1937

The Mummy Chronicles: Heart of the Pharaoh

late 1937

The Mummy Chronicles: The Curse of the Nile **(Alex is 12)**

July 1938

The Mummy Chronicles: Flight of the Phoenix

Sep 1938(e)

The Mummy: Secrets of the Medjai "A New Beginning" (2-part episode)

Nov 1938(e)

The Mummy: Secrets of the Medjai "The Dark Medjai"

Jan 1939(e)

The Mummy: Secrets of the Medjai "Like Father, Like Son"

Feb 1939(e)

The Mummy: Secrets of the Medjai "A Fair to Remember"

Mar 1939(e)

The Mummy: Secrets of the Medjai "The Enemy of My Enemy"

Apr 1939(e)

The Mummy: Secrets of the Medjai "The Cold"

May 1939(e)

The Mummy: Secrets of the Medjai "Time Before Time"

June 1939(e)

The Mummy: Secrets of the Medjai "Spring of Evil"

Jul 1939(e)

The Mummy: Secrets of the Medjai "Old Friends"

Jul 1939(e)

The Mummy: Secrets of the Medjai "Trio"

Aug 1939(e)

The Mummy: Secrets of the Medjai "Just Another Piece of Jewelry"

Aug 1939(e)

The Mummy: Secrets of the Medjai "The Reckoning"

Sep 1939

Outbreak of World War Two.

Late 1939 or early 1940

At age 14 Alex was sent to Australia.

(*The Mummy: Tomb of the Dragon Emperor* novelization)

1939-1945

World War Two. Rick and Evy work for British Intelligence.

(Reference in *The Mummy: Tomb of the Dragon Emperor* (movie))

1940

The Eye of Shangri-La is smuggled out of China.

(Reference in *The Mummy: Tomb of the Dragon Emperor* (movie))

Prior to 1946

Rick (and possibly Evelyn) meets Lord Horwood.

(reference in *The Mummy: The Rise and Fall of Xango's Ax* (comic))

Early 1946 (e)

The Mummy: The Rise and Fall of Xango's Ax

Chinese New Year 1947

The Mummy: Tomb of The Dragon Emperor

1948

The Publication of *Tomb of the Dragon Emperor: Myth and Mystery* by Dr Evelyn O'Connell.(Reference in *The Mummy: Tomb of the Dragon Emperor* novelization)

1950(e)

The Mummy 4

(the ending of *The Mummy Tomb of the Dragon Emperor* sets up this adventure – I am going to presume that the adventure did happen but hasn't been told yet)

2002

"I Stand Alone" music video by Godsmack.

2017

The Dark Universe Mummy.

The Golden Book of Amun-Ra appears.

2020

Oded Fehr Cameo Video.

A much older Ardeth Bay is seen in this video and refers to the events of the Dark Universe Mummy.

The Mummy Scorpion King media

Films

The Mummy (1999)

The Mummy Returns (2001)

The Scorpion King (2002)

The Mummy: Tomb Of the Dragon Emperor (2008)

The Scorpion King 2: Rise of a Warrior (2008)

The Scorpion King 3: The Battle for Redemption (2012)

The Scorpion King 4: Quest for Power (2015)

The Scorpion King: Book of Souls (2018)

TV

The Mummy: The Animated Series 2001–2003

1. The Summoning
2. A Candle in the Darkness
3. Against the Elements
4. The Deep Blue Sea
5. Eruption
6. The Orb of Aten
7. The Black Forest
8. The Cloud People
9. Fear Itself
10. The Boy who would be King
11. Howl
12. The Puzzle
13. The Maze

Season 2 was renamed *The Mummy Secrets of the Medjai*

1. A New Beginning Part 1
2. A New Beginning Part 2
3. The Dark Medjai
4. Like Father, Like Son
5. A Fair to Remember
6. The Enemy of My Enemy
7. The Cold
8. Time Before Time
9. Spring of Evil
10. Old Friends
11. Trio
12. Just Another Piece of Jewelry
13. The Reckoning

Books

Novelizations by Max Allan Collins

The Mummy Novelization (1999)

The Mummy Returns Novelization (2001)

The Scorpion King Novelization (2002)

The Mummy: Tomb of the Dragon Emperor Novelization (2008)

The Mummy

The Mummy Returns

The Scorpion King

The Mummy: Tomb of the Dragon Emperor

Junior Novelizations

The Mummy Junior Novelization (1999)

The Mummy Returns Junior Novelization (2001)

The Mummy: A Junior Novelization by David Levithan

The Mummy Returns: Junior Novelization by John Whitman

Scrapbooks

The Mummy Scrapbook (1999)

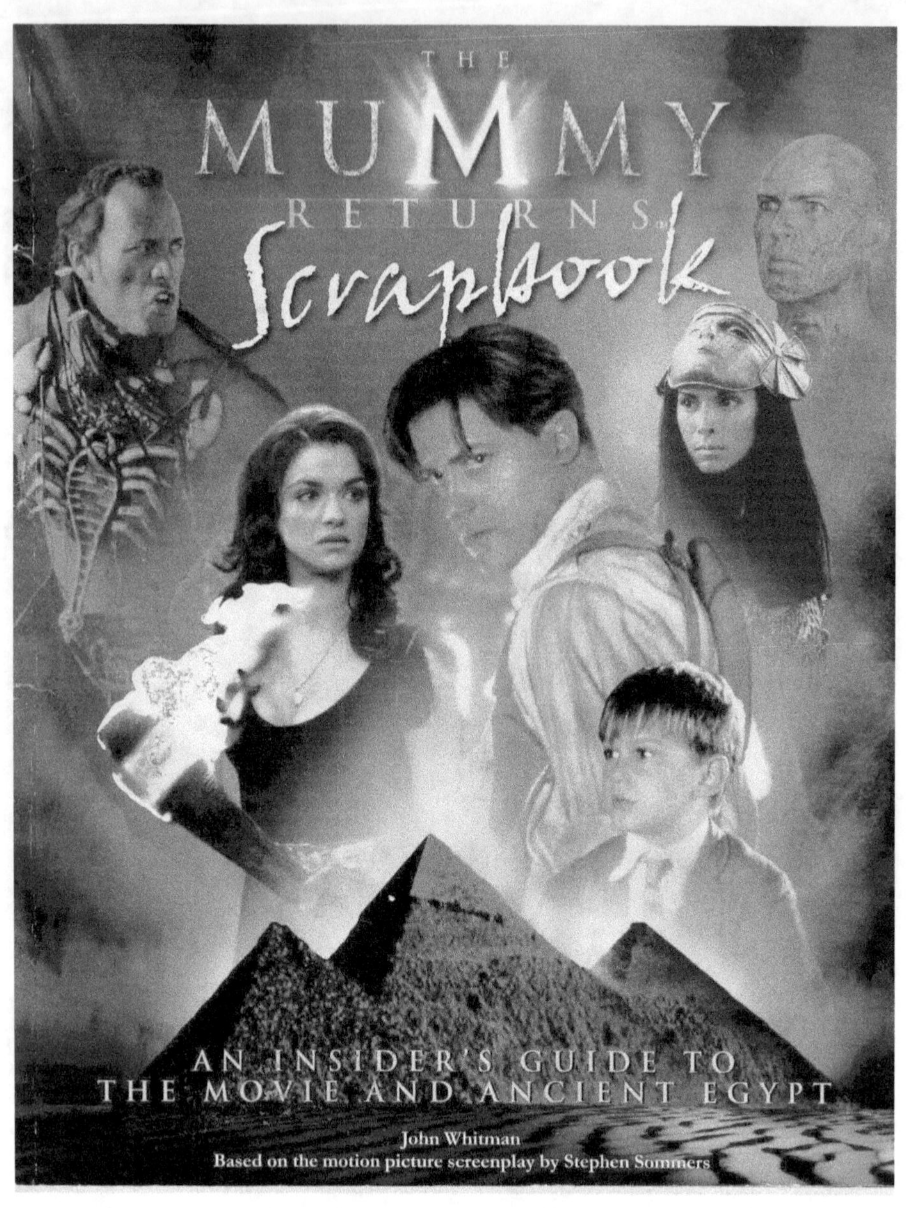

The Mummy Returns Scrapbook (2001)

The Mummy Scrapbook

The Mummy Returns Scrapbook

Penguin Easy Readers

The Mummy Easy Reader (1999)

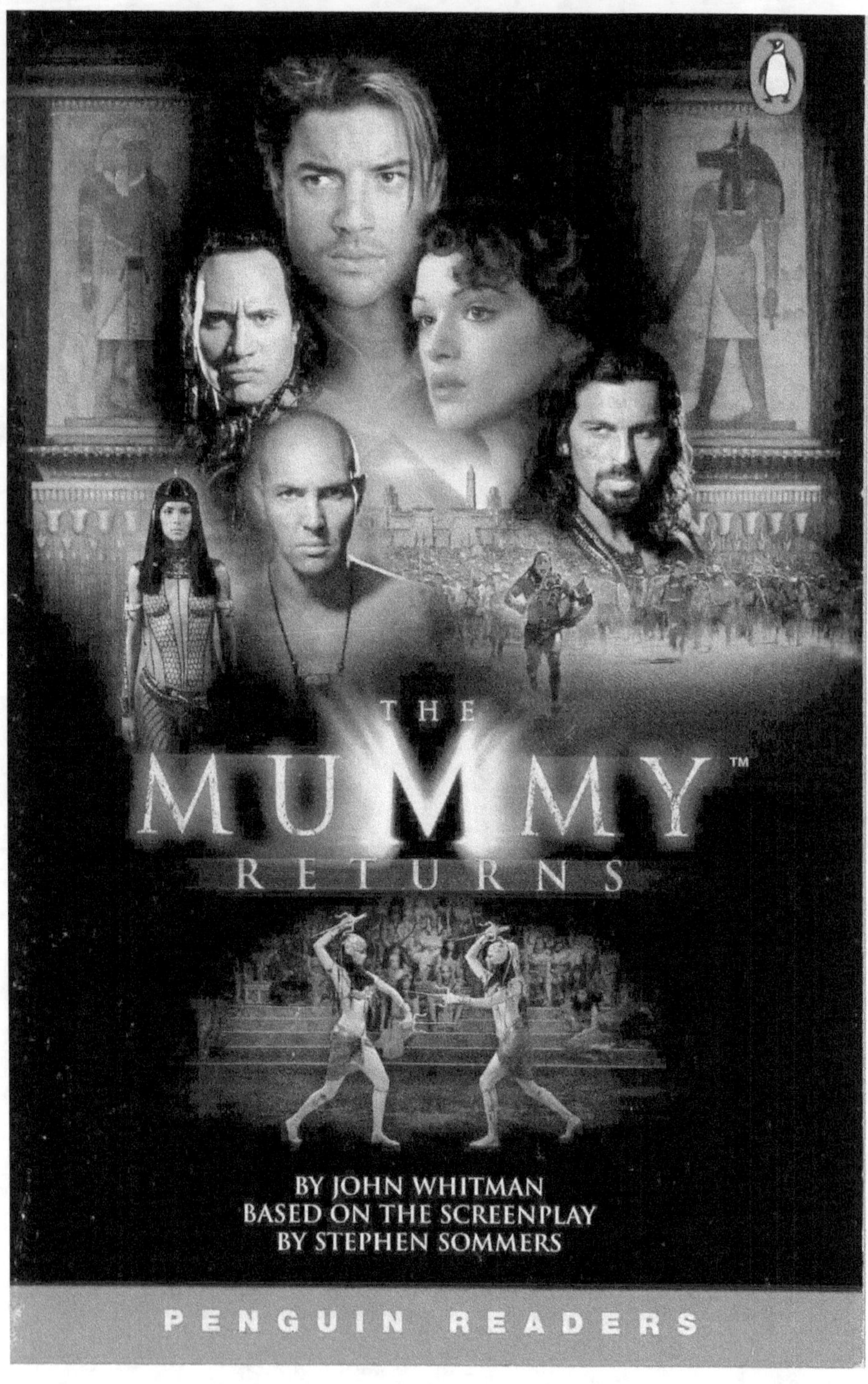

The Mummy Returns Easy Reader (2001)

The Mummy: Against The Element Easy Reader (2003)

The Scorpion King Easy Reader (2002)

The Mummy by Mike Dean

The Mummy Returns by Nancy Taylor

The Mummy: Against the Elements by Lynne Doherty Herndon

The Scorpion King by Andy Hopkins and Jocelyn Po

Scholastic/Helbling Readers

The Mummy: Tomb of the Dragon Emperor Easy Reader (2008)

The Mummy: Tomb of the Dragon Emperor by Jane Revell

Annual

The Mummy Annual (2003)

The Mummy Annual 2003

(Provides Summaries of The Mummy and the Mummy Returns and retells the first three episodes of the Animated Series as short stories)

Original Books

The Mummy Chronicles by Dale Wolverton

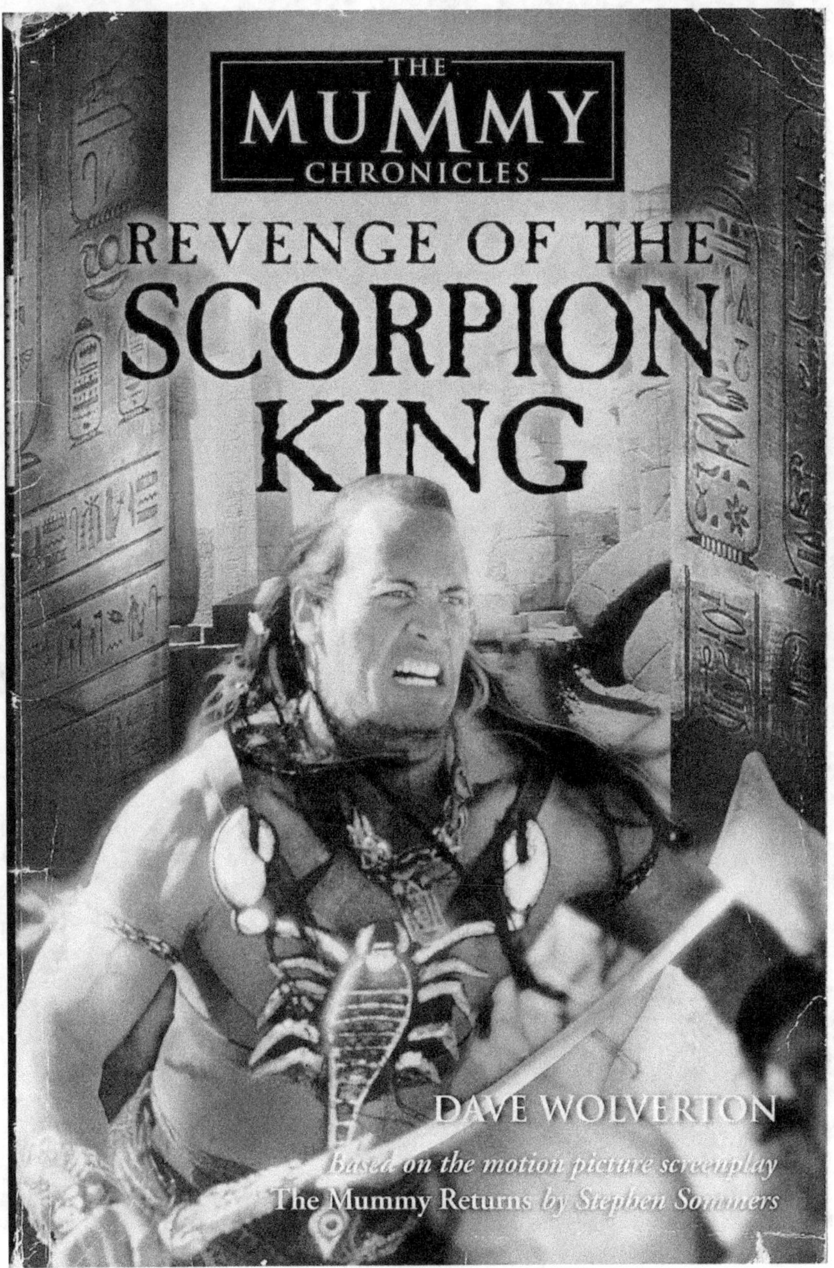

The Mummy Chronicles 1 Revenge of the Scorpion King (2001)

The Mummy Chronicles 2 Heart of the Pharaoh (2001)

The Mummy Chronicles 3 The Curse of the Nile (2001)

The Mummy Chronicles 4 Flight of the Phoenix (2001)

1. *Revenge of The Scorpion King (2001)*
2. *Heart of the Pharaoh (2001)*
3. *The Curse of the Nile (2001)*
4. *Flight of the Phoenix (2001)*

Companion

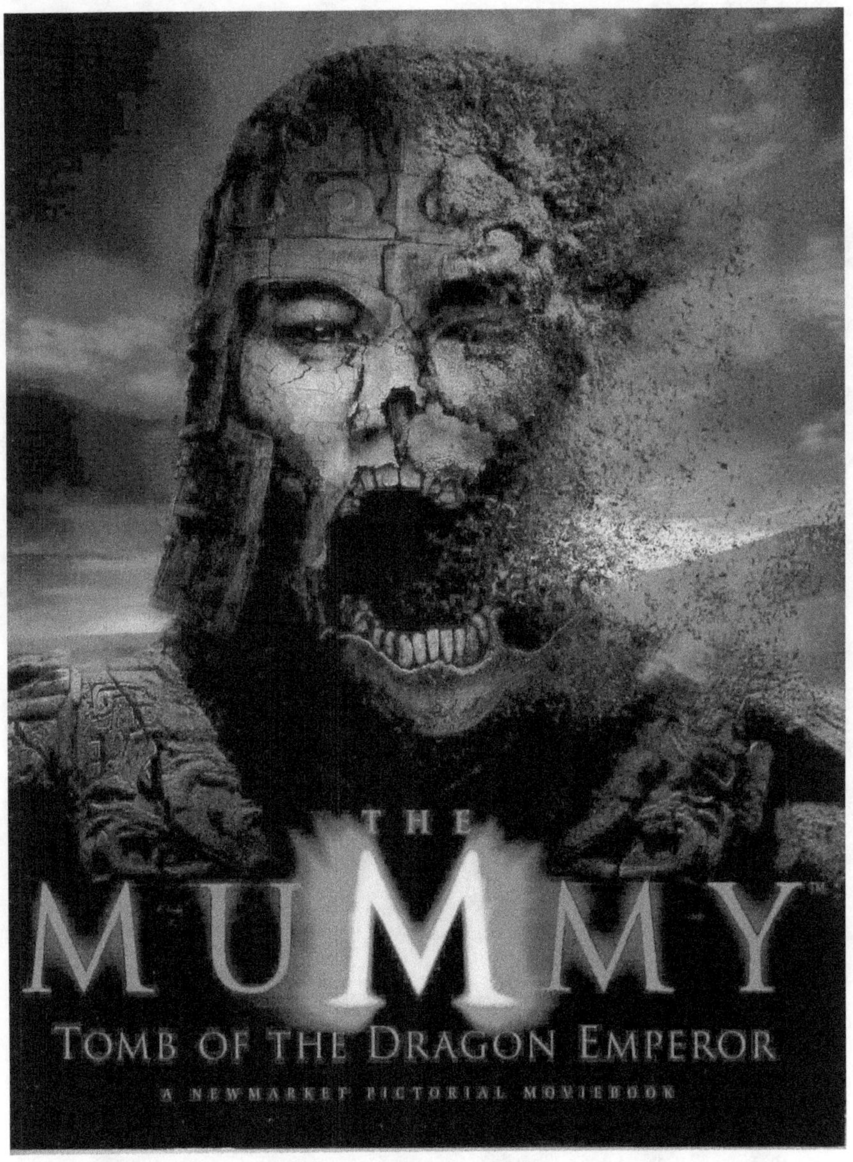

The Mummy: Tomb of the Dragon Emperor A Newmarket Pictorial Movie Book (2008)

The Mummy: Tomb of the Dragon Emperor A Newmarket Pictorial Movie Book

Comics

Chaos Comics

The Mummy: Valley of the Gods #1 (2001)

The Mummy: Valley of the Gods #1

(Only one of the three planned issues was published)

Dark Horse

The Scorpion King: The Akkadian Prophecy Issue 1 (2002)

The Scorpion King: The Akkadian Prophecy Issue 2 (2002)

The Scorpion King: The Akkadian Prophecy #1–2

IDW

The Rise and Fall of Xango's Ax Issue 1 (2008)

The Rise and Fall of Xango's Ax Issue 2 (2008)

The Rise and Fall of Xango's Ax Issue 3 (2008)

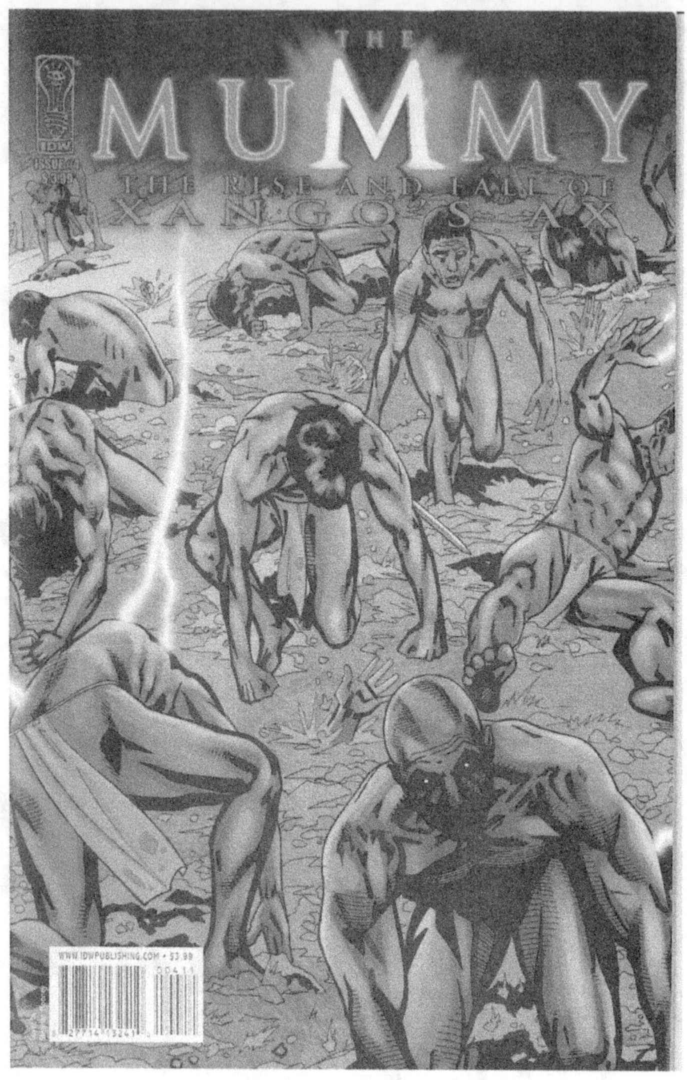

The Rise and Fall of Xango's Ax Issue 4 (2008)

The Mummy: The Rise and Fall of Xango's Ax #1-4

Video Clips

"Forever isn't Long Enough" by Live

"I Stand Alone" by Godsmack

Video Games

The Mummy (2000) for Windows and PlayStation

The Mummy (2000) for Gameboy Color

The Mummy Returns (2001) for PS2

The Mummy Returns (2001) for Gameboy Color

Scorpion King: Rise of the Akkadian (2002) for GameCube and PS2

The Scorpion King: The Rise of the Akkadian PS2 Booklet (2002)

Scorpion King: Sword of Osiris (2002) for Gameboy Advance

The Scorpion King: Sword of Osiris Gameboy Booklet (2002)

The Mummy (2002) for Gameboy Advance

The Mummy: The Animated Series (2004) for PS2

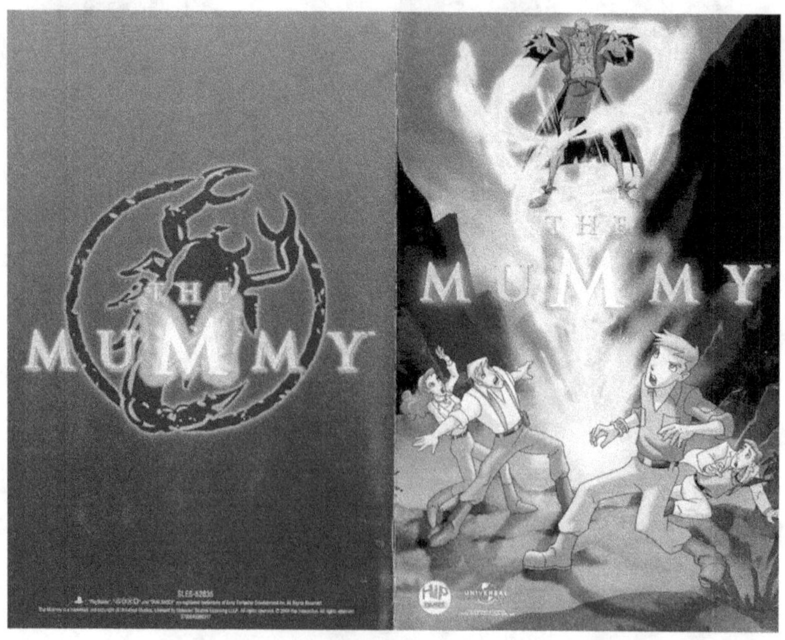

The Mummy PS2 Booklet (2004)

The Mummy (2005) for Java

The Mummy Tomb of the Dragon Emperor (2008) for Nintendo DS, PS2, and Wii

The Mummy Tomb of the Dragon Emperor (2008) for Java

The Mummy Online (2011) MMO for Windows

Theme Park Rides

Revenge of the Mummy

TOYS

The Mummy – Toy Island 1998

12' Figures

> Electronic Mummy
>
> Electronic O'Connell

Figures

> Adventure O'Connell
>
> Legionnaire O'Connell
>
> Decapitated Mummy
>
> Impaled Mummy
>
> Severed Mummy
>
> Cursed Princess
>
> Cursed Imhotep
>
> Cursed Mummy

Playsets

> The Tomb
>
> The Chamber
>
> The Altar with O'Connell and Mummy Princess

Johnny Lightning (1999)

The Mummy Golden Chariot

The Mummy Returns 2001 - Jakks Pacific

Figures

>The Scorpion King

>Imhotep

>Rick O'Connell

>Anck-Su-Namun and Alex O'Connell

>Rick O'Connell and the Pygmy Mummy

Revell

Monster Patrol Mummy Returns Dodge

The Scorpion King 2002 – Jakks Pacific

Figures

>Balthazar

>Cassandra

>Mathayus

>Rock Solid Two-Pack -The Rock and the Scorpion King

The Mummy: The Animated Series 2002 – Taco Bell

>The Manacle of Osiris

>Rick O'Connell Motorcycle

>Alex O'Connell Sidecar with Mummy

>Evy O'Connell coming down a wall

>Puzzling Pyramid

The Mummy: The Animated Series 2002 – KFC (UK)

>Imhotep Awakening

>Rick O'Connell Motorcycle

Alex O'Connell Sidecar with Mummy

Evy O'Connell with a book

Puzzling Pyramid

The Mummy: The Animated Series 2003 – Hardees/Carls Jnr

Alex O'Connell Motorcycle dragging a Mummy

Scarab and Pyramid Game

Mummy Hourglass

Scorpion

Muscle Machines - 2003

The Mummy: The Animated Series Carolina Crusher Truck

The Scorpion King Monster Patrol

The Mummy: The Animated series – Universal/Born to Play

Imhotep

Rick O'Connell

Evy O'Connell

Alex O'Connell

Ardeth Bay

Now Showing 2006 – Sota Toys

Imhotep

Funko Pop – 2021

Imhotep

Rick O'Connell

Evy Carnahan

References

Inspirations

The Mummy **(1932)**

The Mummy (1932)

While the 1999 film was intended as a remake/reboot of the original 1932 movie there are few elements that travel from the original to the remake. Stephen Sommers uses variations of several of the names Ardath Bey/Ardeth Bay, Anck-es-en-Amon/ Anck-Su-Namun and both mummies named Imhotep. To avoid confusion between the two Imhoteps, I have referred to the 1932 mummy as Im-Ho-Tep.

Like the 1999 movie, this movie takes place over three time frames.

730BC Im-Ho-Tep son of the Pharaoh falls in love with Anck-es-en-Amon. After her death, Im-Ho-Tep steals the Scroll of Thoth and buried alive.

1921. Im-Ho-Tep and the Scroll of Thoth are discovered by Sir Joseph Whemple and Ralph Norton. Norton reads from the scroll and resurrects the mummy. Norton is driven insane. Whemple leaves Egypt vowing never to return.

1932. Frank Whemple, Sir Joseph's son, is approached by a man calling himself Ardath Bey who leads them to the tomb of Anck-es-en-Amon. We discover that Bey is Im-Ho-Tep seeking to resurrect his love. Helen Grosvenor, daughter of the Governor of Sudan, is revealed to be the reincarnation of Anck-es-en-Amon.

Im-Ho-Tep tries to awaken the spirit of Anck-es-en-Amon in Helen. The woman repents and seeks the goddess Isis. Im-Ho-Tep is killed and the Scroll burns.

Connections to the 1999 Mummy series:

The Scroll of Thoth is held in the New York Museum as seen in the animated series episode "the Orb of Aten" which is set after this movie.

One wonders at some point between 1921 and 1932 if Ardeth Bay the Medjai from the 1999 Mummy encountered Im-Ho-Tep.

Assuming that Ardeth Bay was not working on the 1921 dig, it is reasonable to assume that reports of the discovery of a mummy named Im-Ho-Tep would certainly have made their way to Dr Terrence Bey, who we know from the 1999 movie is a member of the Medjai and they would have been greatly interested in a resurrected mummy that shared a name with the mummy they were charged to guard.

Either way it seems likely that Ardeth Bay encountered Im-Ho-Tep, and the mummy stole his identity.

Lost Horizon **(1933) novel by James Hilton**

Lost Horizon (1933)

This novel introduced Shangri-La which featured in *The Mummy: Tomb of the Dragon Emperor. Lost Horizon* was made into movies of the same name in 1937 and 1973 with an unofficial version *Bridge of Time* in 1997.

The *Indiana Jones* Franchise (1981-2008)

Indiana Jones in Raiders of the Lost Ark (1981)

This movie series (and spinoff TV, books, and games) popularized the adventuring archeologist brad served as the model for The Mummy franchise.

The *Jungle Book* (1994)

This live action adaptation of Rudyard Kipling's 1894 book of the same name was written and directed by Stephen Sommers. Sam Neil plays Colonel Brydon (an original character for this adaptation) and is the inspiration for Fort Brydon that appears in *The Mummy* (1999).

Tomb Raider (1996- Current)

Lara Croft in *Tomb Raider* Comic

Another popular adventuring archaeologist franchise beginning with a video game. The first movie *Lara Croft: Tomb Raider* (2001) came out the same year as *The Mummy Returns*.

In issues 11& 12 of the Top Cow *Tomb Raider* comic book series released in 2001, Lara visits Shangri-La which was guarded by Yetis like what was seen in *The Mummy: Tomb of the Dragon Emperor*.

Relic Hunter (1999-2001)

Relic Hunter

An adventuring archaeologist TV series featuring Professor Sydney Fox played by Tia Carrere. Interestingly her weapon of choice is a hand crossbow, like the one briefly seen in Rick O'Connell's weapon bag in *The Mummy*.

In "The Emperor's Bride" Season 1 episode 12 (2000), Sydney runs up against fellow relic hunter Dallas Carter played by John Schneider. Schneider provided the voice of Rick O'Connell in *The Mummy: The Animated Series*.

LEGACY AND HOMAGES

Looney Tunes: Back in Action **(2003)**

Looney Tunes: Back in Action (2003)

In this follow up to *Space Jam* (1996), Brendan Fraser plays Damien "D.J." Drake Jnr, a stuntman who also works on the Warner Brothers lot as a security guard, where he meets and interacts with the Looney Tunes. DJ tells Daffy Duck that he worked as a stuntman on *The Mummy* and was in the film more than Brendan Fraser.

Veritas: The Quest **(2003)**

This 13-episode series features the adventures of The Veritas Foundation an archaeological group run by Dr Solomon Zond (Alex Carter) and his son Nikko (Ryan Merriman), and the show is one of Colbie Smother's first roles. Arnold Vosloo (Imhotep in *The Mummy* and *The Mummy Returns*) plays Vincent, their bodyguard. The episode "Mummy Virus" has Vincent making the comment the Mummies are nothing but trouble. A later episode "The Lost Codex" has Nikko commenting that there is always a mummy popping up to Vincent.

Van Helsing **(2004)**

Van Helsing (2004)

Steven Sommers follow up to the Mummy films with a Universal monster mash as Gabriel Van Helsing (Hugh Jackman) battles Mr. Hyde, Frankenstein's monster, Dracula and a wolfman. The movies feature Mummy Alumni, Kevin J. O'Conner (Beni in *The Mummy*), Alun Armstrong (The Curator in *The Mummy Returns*) and future alumni, Will Kemp (Drazen in *The Scorpion King 4: Quest for Power*).

La Tomba (The Tomb) (2004)

La Tomba (The Tomb) (2004)

Directed by Bruno Mattei (credited as David Hunt in some cuts) and filmed in the Philippines. This movie opens in a Mayan temple and the high priest Tatamatli is captured trying to unleash his god Coatlicue and is mummified by his accomplice to return later to try again. We then flash to contemporary Mexico and an archeology class discovers the temple and the body of Tatamatli. The movie not only riffs on *The Mummy* (1999), but it also borrows footage from that movie as well as the *Indiana Jones* and *Evil Dead* series. It was released in the United States as *The Tomb* and reportedly a subsequent reissue was titled *The Mummy 4.*

The Curse of King Tut's Tomb (2006)

The Curse of King Tut's Tomb (2006)

This 2006 miniseries serves as mockbuster version of the Mummy, directed by Russell Mulcahy (*The Scorpion King 2: Rise of a Warrior*).

Filmed in India and set in Egypt, Casper Van Dien plays Danny Freemont, a professor and treasure hunter, who seeks the assistance of Dr Azelia Barakat (Leonor Varela) to King Tut's tomb in 1922, but our adventurers are in a race with Morgan Sinclair, played by Jonathan Hyde an evil version of his character in The Mummy. The movie ends with the discovery of the tomb and battle against evil before time is reset and the discovery is reset to how history recorded the discovery by Howard Carter and Lord Carnavon.

Journey to the Centre of the Earth (2008)

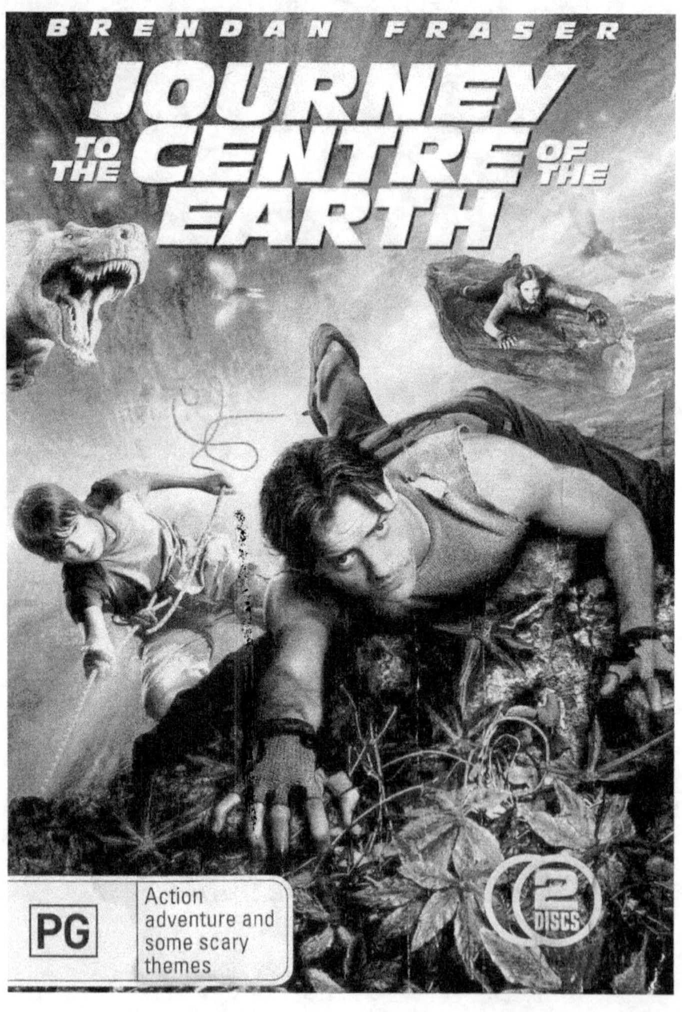

Journey to the Centre of the Earth (2008)

Journey 2: The Mysterious Island (2012)

This updating/sequel to the 1864 Jules Verne novel of the same name starred Brendan Fraser as Trevor Anderson, a geologist who along with his nephew, Sean (Josh Hutcherson) search for his missing brother Max and discover that the Jules Verne novel was based on true events.

A sequel *Journey 2: The Mysterious Island* (2012) has Sean and his stepfather Hank (Dwayne Johnson), searching for Sean's grandfather Alexander Anderson (Michael Caine) and discovering that Jules Verne's *The Mysterious Island* (1875) was also based on true events. *Scorpion King* alumni Branscombe Richmond had a cameo.

G.I. Joe: The Rise of Cobra (2009)

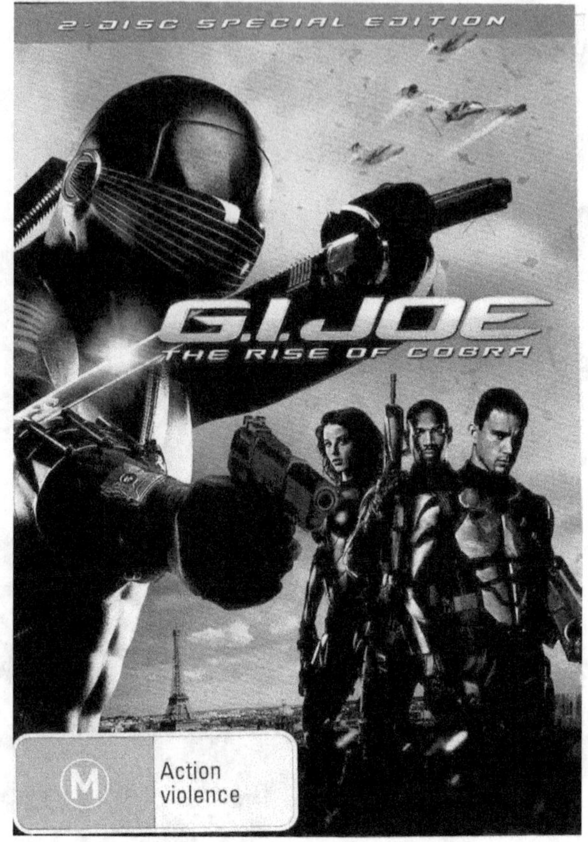

G.I. Joe: The Rise of Cobra (2009)

Directed by Steven Sommers, this film based on the 1980s toy line and associated comic and animated series featured several Mummy alumni including Arnold Vosloo, Adewale Akinnuoye-Agbaje, Kevin J. O'Connell, and Brendan Fraser. Fraser appeared in a cameo playing Sgt Stone. In an article promoting the film "Brendan Fraser geeks out over *G.I. Joe* Cameo" by Fred Topel, he states "I made a personal choice when I arrived and kind of ripped it off and decided I'd be some sort of hybrid of a great-great-grandson of Rick O'Connell."

Leverage "The Second David Job" Season 1 Episode 13 (2009)

The Leverage team rob the Blackpoole Gallery of a Museum. Erick Avari (Doctor Terrence Bey) plays Dr Darian Lloyd director of the

Museum. The team convince him that the mummy in the museum is cursed so that he will send the mummy to the basement to aid their plan.

Castle "Wrapped Up in Death" Season 2 Episode 19 (2010)

Castle and Beckett investigate the murder of an archeologist. The victim had returned from Mexico after discovering the mummy of a Mayan King. Erick Avari plays Rupert Bentley the financier for the expedition who claims that it was the curse of the Mummy

The Mummy Resurrected (2014)

The Mummy Resurrected (2014) with original logo

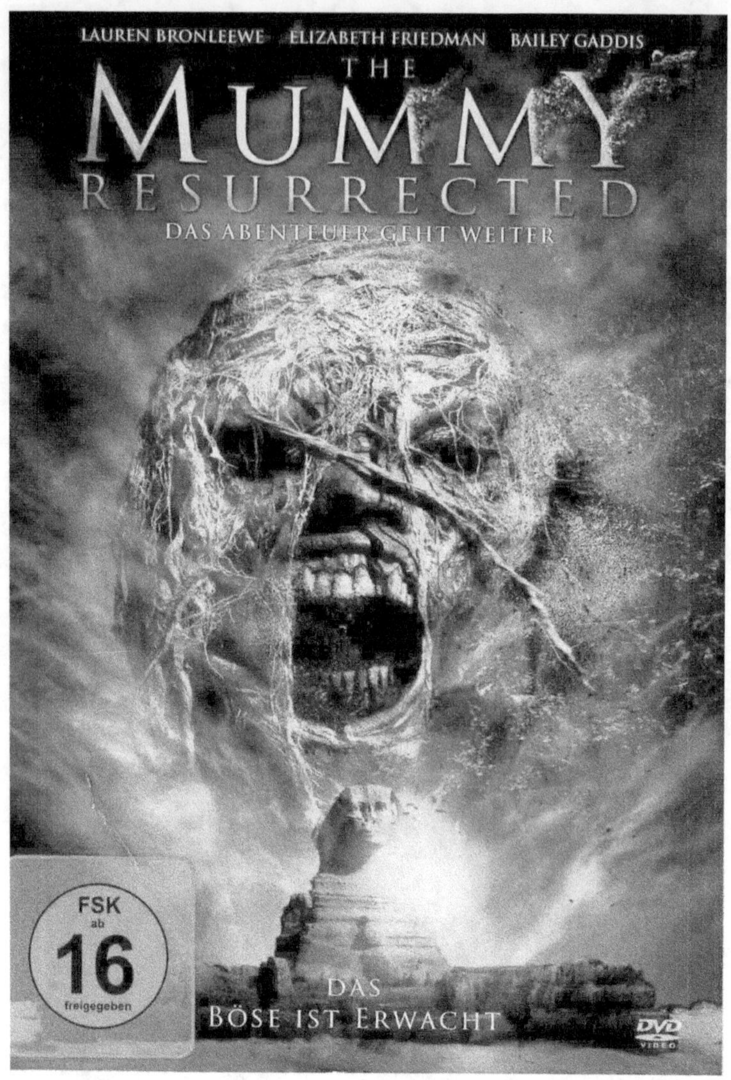

The Mummy Resurrected (2014) with revised logo

This 2014 movie from Still Night Monster Movies, another unofficial version of Bram Stoker's *Jewel of the Seven Stars* (1903) in its original release had "Mummy" written in the same style as the Mummy trilogy to create the illusion that this was another movie in that cycle (previous page) – later releases changed the title font (above).

The title *The Mummy Resurrected* also implied this was a return for the series, as did the 2019 movies *The Mummy Reborn* (High Octane Pictures) and *The Mummy Rebirth* (Uncork'd Entertainment).

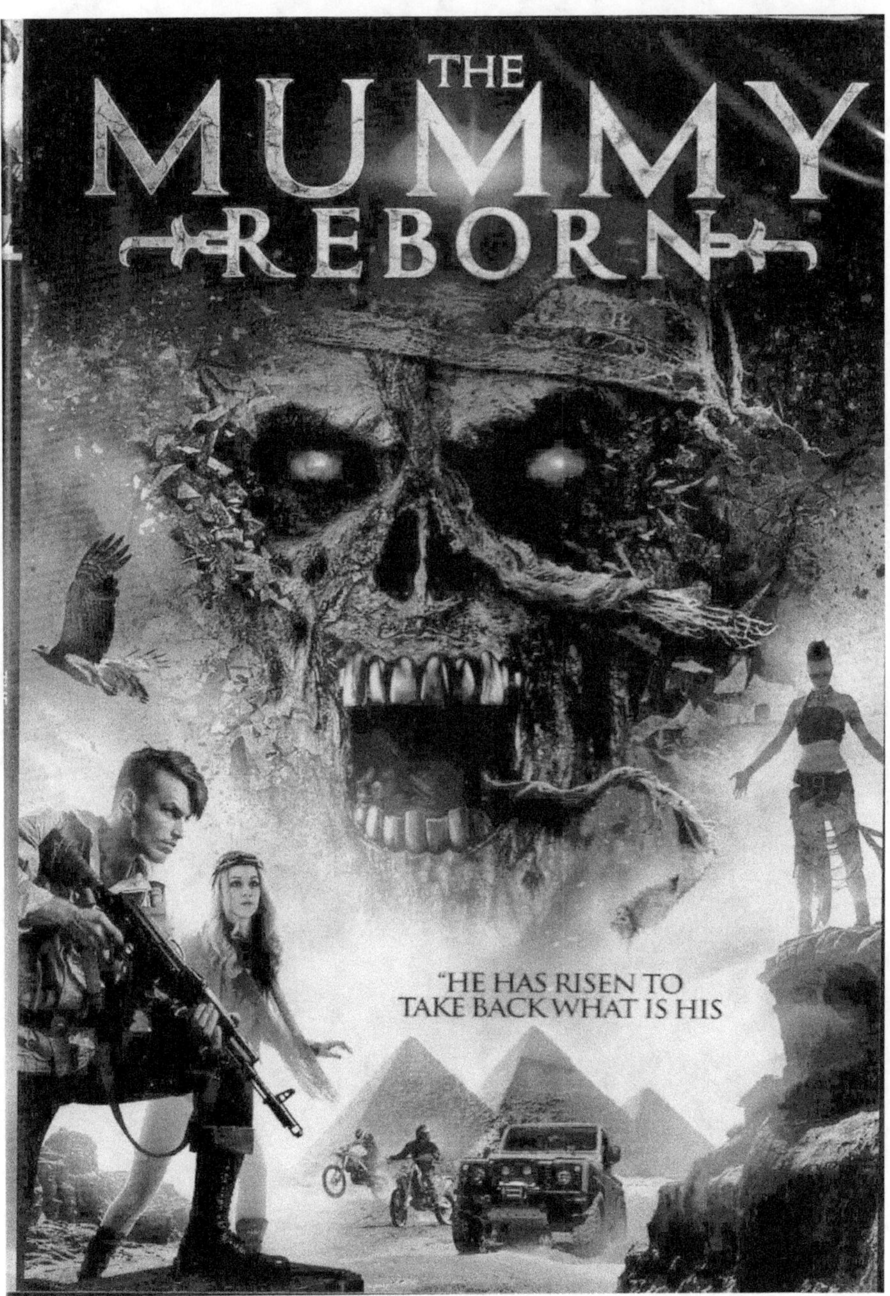

The Mummy Reborn (2019)

The Mummy Rebirth (2019)

Hercules **(2014)**

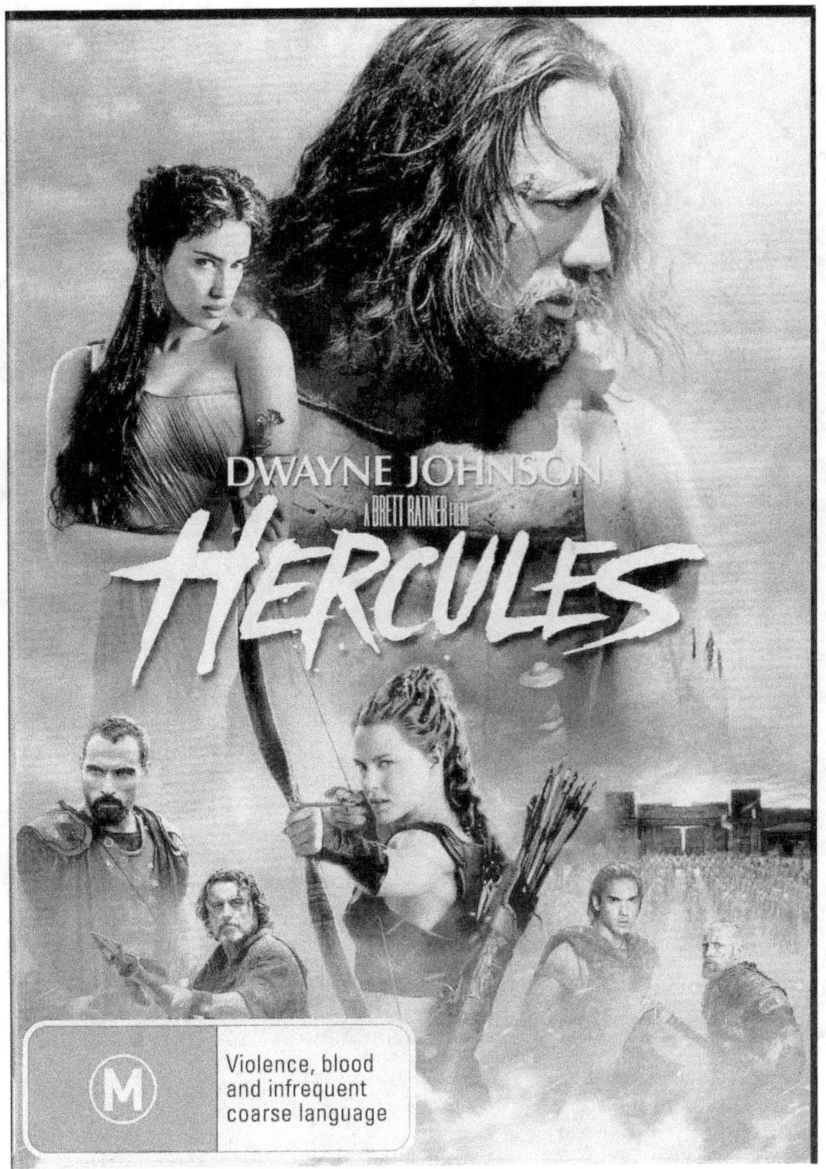

Hercules (2014)

Between *The Scorpion King 3: Battle for Redemption* (2012) and *The Scorpion King 4: Quest for Power* (2015) both starring Victor Webster, The Rock returned to the sword and sorcery genre playing the title role of Hercules.

Dark Universe: The Mummy **(2017)**

The Mummy (2017)

The first movie in what was to be the Dark Universe, has an appearance of the golden Book of the Amun-Ra.

Other than that, there appears to be no connection to any of the earlier Mummy films.

The monster hunting organization Prodigium appears to have no connection to the Medjai.

Blood & Treasure **TV Series (2019-Current)**

This series features former FBI agent Danny McNamara and Egyptian born thief Lexi Vaziri travelling the world searching for the stolen body of Cleopatra racing a terrorist Karim Farouk (Oded Fehr) who seeks to use the body to create a bioweapon.

In this series there are several possible connections between *Blood and Treasure* and *The Mummy* series.

Firstly, the series revolves around the discovery of the Tomb of Antony and Cleopatra. In *The Mummy Chronicles: Heart of the Pharaoh* during 1937 Alex O'Connell prevented Italian forces from looting the Tomb of Antony and Cleopatra. *Blood & Treasure* reveals that the tomb had previously been moved before Nazi Soldiers had taken the body of Cleopatra in 1942. It is likely that the tomb was moved to the pyramid seen in *Blood & Treasure* after that the events of *Heart of the Pharoah*.

In *Blood & Treasure*, Cleopatra's tomb is guarded by the Brotherhood of Serapis, a group founded by the children of Cleopatra to protect her tomb. Given that their mission has much in common with the Medjai of the Mummy, one wonders if they were an offshoot or one of the tribes of the Medjai.

When asked about how the Nazis were able to invade the tomb in 1942 it is mentioned that they lost many people in the war. Implicitly the reference is to World War Two but if the Brotherhood were part of the Medjai then they would still have been recovering from losses in the battle against the army of Anubis seen in the *Mummy Returns*.

The third connection comes from the terrorist Karim Farouk - we discover that his real name is Rashid Higazi and that he was a former Brotherhood agent. More than that he bears a remarkable resemblance to Ardeth Bay of the Medjai. (This is because Oded Fehr plays both men). I'm assuming that Higazi was born around 1970 (like Fehr) which would make him most likely the grandson or great grandson of Bay.

Finding 'Ohana **(2021)**

This Netflix original movie, starred *Scorpion King* alumni Branscombe Richmond and Kelly Hu. A family friendly adventure, with callbacks to *Indiana Jones* and *The Goonies*, has Hu's children searching for a lost treasure to save their grandfather's property.

Jungle Cruise (2021)

Jungle Cruise (2021)

Based on the Disney theme park ride of the same name riverboat captain Frank Wolff (Dwayne "The Rock" Johnson), helps sister and brother academics, Lily and McGregor Houghton find a mystical artefact. Many reviews referred to the movie as "*The Mummy Lite.*"

Bibliography

Adler, S. (2008) "'Mummy 4' to Re-Locate to Latin America with a New Twist, Says Director" https://www.mtv.com/news/2430450/mummy-4-to-re-locate-to-latin-america-with-new-twist-says-director/

Allie, S. et al (2002) The Scorpion King: The Akkadian Prophecy (1) Dark Horse Comics

Allie, S. et al (200(2) The Scorpion King: The Akkadian Prophecy (2) Dark Horse Comics

Alvar, N. (2021) "Disney's Jungle Cruise is Basically the Mummy" https://culturedvultures.com/disney-jungle-cruise-is-basically-the-mummy/

Baron, R. (2021) "Clive Barker Details His Plans for a Transgender Mummy Remake" https://www.cbr.com/clive-barker-mummy-remake-transgender/

Brehmer, N. (2017) "Script to Pieces: Clive Barker's The Mummy" https://wickedhorror.com/features/script-pieces-clive-barkers-mummy/

Brooks, N. (2021) "The Mummy is the Pinnacle of Action Horror" https://www.cbr.com/why-the-mummy-best-action-horror/

Bussey, B. (2017) "The Mummy: Four Movies Which Never Got Made" The Mummy: four movies which never got made (yahoo.com)

Cohen, R. (Director) (2008) *The Mummy: Tomb of the Dragon Emperor* [film] Universal Pictures

Collins, M.A. (1999) *The Mummy* Ebury Press

Collins, M.A. (2001) *The Mummy Returns* Berkley Boulevard Books

Collins, M.A. (2008) *The Mummy: The Tomb of the Dragon Emperor* Berkley Boulevard Books

Collins. M.A. (2002) *The Scorpion King* Berkley Boulevard Books

Cotter, C. (2020) "The Mummy Franchise Timeline: When All the Movies Take Place" https://screenrant.com/mummy-movies-in-order-timeline/

Cowie, S. & Johnson T. (2002) *The Mummy in Fact, Fiction and Film* McFarland & Company

Dean, M. (1999) *The Mummy* Penguin

Downey, A. et al (1999) *The Mummy: The Complete Movie Scrapbook* Scholastic

Elliott, M. (Director) (2014) *The Scorpion King 4: Quest for Power* Universal 1440 Entertainment

Ferguson, M. (2021) "What the Unmade Brendan Fraser The Mummy 4 Would Have been About" https://screenrant.com/mummy-4-movie-brendan-fraser-story-rise-astecs/)

Garris, M. (2021) "Clive Barker" *Post Mortem with Mick Garris* Episode 119 Aired April 20, 2021, Spotify

Ghosh, M. (2021) "Will Mummy 4 Ever Happen? Rachel Weisz and Brendan Fraser Talks About the Franchise." https://stanfordartsreview.com/2021/02/08/will-mummy-4-ever-happen-rachel-weisz-and-brendan-fraser-talks-about-the-franchise/

Herndon, L.D. (2003) *The Mummy: Against The Elements* Penguin

Hutchinson, S (2020)" The Mummy Returns:10 Behind the Scenes Facts About the Sequel" https://screenrant.com/mummy-returns-sequel-behind-scenes-facts/

Jabcuga, J. et al (2008) *The Mummy: The Rise and Fall of Xango's Ax (1)* IDW Publishing

Jabcuga, J. et al (2008) *The Mummy: The Rise and Fall of Xango's Ax (2)* IDW Publishing

Jabcuga, J. et al (2008) *The Mummy: The Rise and Fall of Xango's Ax (3)* IDW Publishing

Jabcuga, J. et al (2008) *The Mummy: The Rise and Fall of Xango's Ax (4)* IDW Publishing

Kennedy, M. (2020) "The Mummy Returns: Rick and Evy's Son Created a Plot Hole" https://screenrant.com/mummy-movies-in-order-timeline/

Kroll, J. (2020) "'Scorpion King' Reboot In Works From Dwayne Johnson And Dany Garcia's Seven Bucks Productions And Universal; 'Straight Outta Compton' Scribe Jonathan Herman Penning Script" https://deadline.com/2020/11/dwayne-johnson-scorpion-king-straight-outta-compton-jonathan-herman-1234611341/

Levithan, D. (1999) *The Mummy: A Junior Novelization* Scholastic

Lillejord, K. (2020) 10 behind-the-scenes facts about the Mummy https://screenrant.com/mummy-1999-behind-scenes-facts-trivia/

Milligan, P. et al (2017) *The Mummy: Palimpsest* Titan Books

Mulcahy, R. (Director) (2008) *The Scorpion King 2: Rise of a Warrior* Universal Home Entertainment

The Mummy Annual 2003 (2002) Pedigree

The Mummy: Tomb of the Dragon Emperor A Newmarket Pictorial Movie Book (2008) Newmarket

Paul, D.M. (Director) (2018) *The Scorpion King: Book of Souls* [film] Universal 1440 Entertainment

Reckmann, N. (2021) "Jungle Cruise desperately want to be the Mummy and Failed" https://gamerant.com/jungle-cruise-the-mummy-failed/

Reine, R. (Director) (2012) *The Scorpion King 3: Battle for Redemption* [film] Universal 1440 Entertainment

Revell, J. (2009) *The Mummy: Tomb of the Dragon Emperor* Scholastic

Reyes, M. (2019) "It's Time for The Mummy 4 To Be Resurrected" https://www.cinemablend.com/news/2482105/its-time-for-the-mummy-4-to-be-resurrected

Russell, C. (Director) (2002) *The Scorpion King* [film] Universal Pictures

Schnelbach, L. (2020) "Celebrating the Chaotic Energy of The Mummy" https://www.tor.com/2020/11/12/celebrating-the-chaotic-energy-of-the-mummy/

Sommers, S. (Director) (1999) *The Mummy* [film] Universal Pictures

Sommers, S. (Director) (2001) *The Mummy Returns* [film] Universal Pictures

Sommers, S. (Executive Producer) (2001-2003) *The Mummy: The Animated Series* [TV Series] Freemantle Media International, Medium Rare Entertainment, Universal Studios.

Spinks, A. (2010) "The Mummy 3 Star Says the Mummy 4 is Happening" https://www.thehollywoodnews.com/2010/10/30/mummy-3-star-mummy-4-happening/

Squires, J. (2017) "George Romero and Clive Barker Almost Directed 'The Mummy' Remakes in the 90s" https://bloody-disgusting.com/movie/3441008/george-romero-clive-barker-almost-directed-mummy-remakes-90s/

Stevenson, J. (2009) "Here Are Some of the Rumors. And Who Should Direct Sommers or Cohen?" https://mummy42010.blogspot.com/

Sum, E. (2021) "RIP The Mummy (1999–2008) Retrospective" https://otakunoculture.com/2017/05/05/themummy1999-2008retrospective/

Taylor, N. (2001) *The Mummy Returns* Penguin

Whitman, J (2001) *The Mummy Returns Scrapbook: An Insider's Guide to the Movie and Ancient Egypt* Corgi Yearling Books

Whitman, J. (2001) *The Mummy Returns* Corgi Yearling Books

Wolfman, M & Broome, M. (2001) *The Mummy: Valley of the Gods (1)* Chaos! Comics

Wolverton, D (2001) *The Mummy Chronicles 1: Revenge of the Scorpion King* Corgi Yearling Books

Wolverton, D (2001) *The Mummy Chronicles 2: Heart of the Pharaoh* Bantam Books

Wolverton, D (2001) *The Mummy Chronicles 3: The Curse of the Nile* Bantam Books

Wolverton, D (2001) *The Mummy Chronicles 4: Flight of the Phoenix* Bantam Books.

Websites

www.imdb.com

https://mummy.fandom.com/wiki/Main_Page   Rickipedia: The Mummy Wiki.

http://mummy.popapostle.com/ "Pop Apostle Mummy/Scorpion King Studies"

https://zenade.angelfire.com/mummy/chronicles.html   "The Chronology"

www.ingramcontent.com/pod-product-compliance
Lightning Source LLC
Chambersburg PA
CBHW060905140726
47996CB00001B/124